This *Handbook for Participants* is designed specifically for those who are going to be involved in the Care Ministry of their congregations.

An additional *Handbook for Pastors and Leaders* is available and includes the same material as the *Handbook for Participants* but with the addition of Section 2, which contains all the supplemental material. All who attend a *Care Pastors Training Conference* should have a copy of either of these *Handbooks*.

THE CARE REVOLUTION HANDBOOK
FOR PARTICIPANTS

Step-By-Step Directions for Implementing An Effective Care Ministry

by
DR. JOHN W. BOSMAN

EQUIP PRESS
Colorado Springs

THE CARE REVOLUTION HANDBOOK
FOR PARTICIPANTS
Step-By-Step Directions for Implementing an Effective Care Ministry

Copyright © 2019 Dr. John W. Bosman

All rights reserved. No part of this publication may be reproduced, distributed, or transmitted in any form or by any means, without prior written permission.

Scripture quotations marked (ESV) are taken from The ESV® Bible (The Holy Bible, English Standard Version®) copyright © 2001 by Crossway, a publishing minis-try of Good News Publishers. ESV® Text Edition: 2011. The ESV® text has been reproduced in cooperation with and by permission of Good News Publishers. Unauthorized reproduction of this publication is prohibited. Used by permission. All rights reserved.

Scripture quotations marked (KJV) are taken from the King James Bible. Accessed on Bible Gateway at www.BibleGateway.com.

Scripture quotations marked (NASB) are taken from the New American Standard Bible® (NASB), copyright © 1960, 1962, 1963, 1968, 1971, 1972, 1973, 1975, 1977, 1995 by The Lockman Foundation, www.Lockman.org. Used by permission.

Scripture quotations marked (NIV) are taken from the Holy Bible, New International Version. Copyright © 1973, 1978, 1984, 2011 by Biblica, Inc.® Used by permission. All rights reserved worldwide.

Scripture quotations marked (NKJV) are taken from the New King James Version®. Copyright © 1982 by Thomas Nelson, Inc. Used by permission. All rights reserved.

Scripture quotations marked (NLT) are taken from the Holy Bible, New Living Translation, copyright © 1996, 2004, 2015 by Tyndale House Foundation. Used by permission of Tyndale House Publishers, Inc., Carol Stream, Illinois 60188. All rights reserved.

Scripture quotations marked (NRSV) are taken from the New Revised Standard Version Bible, copyright © 1989 the Division of Christian Education of the National Council of the Churches of Christ in the United States of America. Used by permission. All rights reserved.

First Edition: Year 2019
The Care Revolution / Dr. John W. Bosman
Paperback ISBN: 978-1-951304-03-4
ebook ISBN: 978-1-951304-04-1

DEDICATION

This *Handbook* is affectionately dedicated to the scores of steadfast pastors, leaders, and faithful men and women across the United Sates of America and South Africa who have diligently put into practice the principles and systems of the *Care Revolution* — especially those who were willing to test the concept in a pilot program. You are the brave pioneers who have brought reality to the *Care Revolution*.

My sincere thanks and appreciation go to the Fontenot family of Lake Charles, Louisiana, who have made this project possible in memory of their patriarch, James Fontenot.

INTRODUCTION

The *Handbook* is designed to be an implementation companion to my book, *The Care Revolution*. If you have not yet done so, I highly recommend that you read it first to gain comprehensive insight into the workings of member-run care ministry. In the *Care Revolution*, I deal with the philosophical, theological, and theoretical aspects of *why* we need a new paradigm for pastoral care and, furthermore, extensively reference the modern-day demands pastors and church leaders face.

Out of these realities, we have designed a very workable system called the *Care Ministry Network*. I fully describe the functions and implementation of the system in this handbook you are now reading. The *Care Ministry Network* is a proven system of congregational care that provides a safety net for churches to prevent people from falling through the cracks and simultaneously close the proverbial backdoor, so people won't slip through it unknowingly.

Care Revolution is undergirded by Scripture and is packed with numerous Bible references and direct verse quotes. In addition to these singular references, one entire chapter in that book is devoted entirely to Scriptural underpinning.

The premise of the *Care Revolution* is based on the persuasion that:
- (i) the pastor cannot do ministry alone, and should not,
- (ii) the traditional model of providing pastoral care is antiquated and no longer works,
- (iii) ministry is not intended only for a select few and this faulty practice needs to be transformed,
- (iv) every believer is a minister and deserves to be equipped for works of service,
- (v) caring for God's people should be part of a church's discipling process, and
- (vi) pastors are the ones responsible for the equipping and developing of believers.

Value of Systems

Oftentimes, people say that "we don't need systems or programs in the church today." Well, I cannot vouch for the validity of programs, because I know programs may attract people, but do not necessarily keep them. When it comes to *systems*, however, that is a different story. Every living body needs systems to exist and grow. The human body, I am told, functions on eleven different systems and cannot do without a single one of them. If any one of these systems fails, disease sets into the body. When that happens, one of the first symptoms is lack of energy. The body cannot then function as it should.

The Church is not a system, but needs systems to be able to function. We have, in the past, focused our attention on numerical growth and additional ministries at the cost of healthy and necessary systems. We then wonder why the church remains incapacitated. It does not help much to reach out to people via social media and other means and then not have a system whereby we can connect with them. We may add *numbers*, but we won't gain *members*.

The care system we advocate is referred to as the *Care Ministry Network*, which is the local church expression of *The Care Revolution*. At the heart of developing an authentic care system in a congregation, is the creation of a culture of care where love and acceptance become an outflow of who the church really is. I often refer to a church's culture as its *default position*. Culture describes what the church thinks, and who they truly are at heart. If a church's culture is vested in love, acceptance, and genuine care, they will always default to it as a body. It's not so much about *doing* as it is about *being*.

> "God composed the body, having given greater honor to that part which lacks it, that there should be no schism in the body, *but that the members should have the same care for one another*. And if one member suffers, all the members suffer with it; or if one member is honored, all the members rejoice with it" (1 Corinthians 12:24-26. Italics by author).

Cultivating a culture of care requires genuine love and concern among church members and extends to all they touch. This is the way spiritual health is generated and an atmosphere of unity is set for concentrated prayer, evangelism, outreach, missions, etc. Without loving each other as Jesus expects, the church simply cannot be effective in any of its spiritual obligations.

> The love of God
> must flow down
> the aisles of our church
> before it will flow down
> the streets of our city.

Thinking of the *Care Ministry Network* as an added-on program will most certainly take away from its intent. We do not simply look at it as a group of people helping their pastor, but rather as cultivating an atmosphere whereby everyone becomes involved in making it happen. Our care system should be an outflow of the created culture where all members "love their neighbor as themselves."

Through the Care Ministry Network, we purpose to basically fulfill the following:
1. Help people discover and develop their spiritual gifts.
2. Release people to function according to their giftedness.
3. Empower church members to care for one another.
4. Provide a network of care that reaches all members of the congregation.
5. Significantly close the proverbial "back door".
6. Cultivate a culture of care in the church (which is more than a program).
7. Be a catalyst in promoting spiritual maturity.

The Practical Handbook

In this *Handbook*, I am going to deal with the practical implementation of the *Care Ministry Network* as it pertains to *The Care Revolution*. I like to say it this way: While the *Care Revolution* explains the WHY, the *Handbook* clarifies the HOW. For continuity's sake, it may be necessary at times to repeat a statement or a truth out of *Care Revolution* to substantiate what we are dealing with in the *Handbook*. I will not, however, simply restate any information just for repetition's sake.

The *Handbook* is the culmination of several pilot programs that have been applied in different churches over several years of trials and errors and comes to the reader as a proven guidebook and valuable resource. It is not intended only to assist leaders when they *equip* their workers, but also to serve as a *continuous road map* for those involved in care ministry after they have been trained. People only remember so much of what they hear during a lecture. Once the training conference is over, they often struggle to recall the complete details of the information they received. Having a manual such as this solves that problem and makes the answers readily available. For that reason, *each person* attending the training conference should have a copy of this handbook in-hand for personal use. Over and above this handbook, we also utilize a *Participant Training Guide*. It draws its information from the *Care Revolution* text book, as well as the *Care Revolution Handbook* in summary form.

My Approach

In the initial portion of the *Handbook*, I will lay the foundation for the crucial need of an authentic care ministry. Not only will this help pastors and leaders to sensibly enter the runway of launching the ministry, it will simultaneously provide an overall perspective to church members who are ready to board the flight of this exciting journey.

I include some introductory remarks concerning the concept itself in the opening chapters. I certainly do not want to insult those who have already read the *Care Revolution* by repeating unnecessary information, so, these explanations are specifically for the benefit of those who may have never been exposed to any insights of the care ministry model and the new paradigm for pastoral care I propose. It is also possible that someone may get this book in hand before reading the *Care Revolution* and may find it difficult to grasp the concepts. By reading these introductory chapters, it will help people get their toes in the water and sense the passion to care for others as well.

My foremost objective remains to provide clear and easy-to-understand direction to pastors, leaders, and church members as they set out to implement and maintain an effective care ministry within their congregation. I have tried to make this book very practical and easily understood so all who study it will be able to effortlessly follow the directives.

Training Conference

No one should ever be involved in the work of the ministry without proper preparation. For that reason, we underscore the importance of those who desire to become involved in care ministry to attend a *Care Pastors Training Conference.* The information contained in this book forms the underlying guidelines with which to equip them. Furthermore, it serves as a very helpful continuation instrument as they fulfill the ministry. The importance of this aspect is understood when we take into consideration that when people are at first being trained to function as Care Pastors, they often receive answers to questions they do not even yet know exist. As they implement the ministry, questions inevitably arise. That is when the information contained in this handbook becomes invaluable.

Once I start rolling out the concept to its full extent, I meticulously take the reader through each step and carefully explain every principle in thorough detail. I have purposely chosen to take on this approach so that pastors and involved members will be able to understand and fully grasp what to do in each step of the application. This is especially important when the Care Pastor training is being done *in-house* by the pastor or one of the leaders of the church. Everyone should be able to find answers in this book to most questions they may have as they apply and continue this ministry.

Many people also find the *Handbook* a great source from which to glean fresh ideas, even after they have been functioning in the care ministry for some time. Every step, every principle, every expectation, is dealt with prudently, just as though I was in the room with you.

If you are serious about caring for others (and I believe you are), you will find this book to be worth its weight in gold.

Clarification

1. Since the *Care Ministry Network* basically relates to *shepherding*, we find it necessary to state emphatically that our Care Ministry Network and its supposition has no resemblance or relationship to the *Shepherding Movement* of several years ago and should not be confused with it at all. Our care ministry is in no way to be identified with any aspects of that movement of the seventies and eighties.

2. The *Care Ministry Network* is a system of care provided by church members to one another and does not include any form of personal authority or manipulation. It is based on sound Biblical principles and healthy ethics. The concept does not allow anyone to usurp authority, nor does it create a setting for anyone to take a group to start their own church.

3. The concept of the *Care Ministry Network* is not intended to make the local church turn inward or become ingrown. It does not propose a turning away

from winning the lost, making disciples, or being the *Ecclesia,* it was meant to be. Instead, its objective is to build a healthy body of believers with an attitude of Christ that compels them to go out and evangelize the world; and, when the unsaved come into the church, they can witness that *these must be disciples of Christ, because they have love one for another.*

CONTENTS

	Introduction	7
	Actual Testimonies From Pastors	17

Section 1 *Implementation Guidelines*

1.	The Pastor Cannot Do It Alone	27
2.	The Essence of Congregational Care	49
3.	Developing the Care Ministry Network	67
4.	Putting the Network Together	75
5.	The Role of the Care Pastor	93
6.	The Contact System	105
7.	The Sunday Connection	127
8.	Further Contacts	141
9.	Some Practical Logistics	153
10.	Acting Professionally	169
11.	Keeping the Vision Alive	187

ACTUAL TESTIMONIES FROM PASTORS
Who Have Implemented The Care Ministry Network In Their Churches[1]

The Care Ministry Network functions well during the good times as well as the tough times. It's effective in small churches as well as large churches. It's applicable in rural as well as suburban and urban areas. It's Biblical and absolutely adaptable.

A Rural Church

The Care Ministry Network has been a tremendous blessing to our church in numerous ways. It has given us a plan and a strategy that allows us to have ongoing/long-term care for every member of our congregation. Also, it has given each Care Pastor a great sense of responsibility and ownership as they help to tend the flock, not to mention it has helped the congregation to feel they are cared for and loved. The Care Ministry Network has taken a huge burden off of the shoulders of the staff knowing that each member is receiving more than just crisis care. This system is a tool that every church needs to implement.

— Pastor Cody

---

[1] Bosman, John W. Care Revolution, Equip Press, Colorado Springs, CO 2018, pp. 211-218.

A Younger Church

This report, on the other hand, comes from a relatively young church that needed a system to reach all their people:

> We have been using the Care Ministry Network model for our pastoral care for about 18 months. It has been amazing how God has helped us to effectively care for the people of our church as we have implemented this great care model. We have continued to add new Care Pastors and deepen the training for the ones we have. For the first time, we see active body ministry, and our people sense genuine care. As a pastor, I cannot express how it has helped to lighten the load and allow me to give my attention to other pressing matters. I honestly believe there has never been a time in the sixteen-year history of our church when our people have received better care. Thank you, Dr. Bosman, for introducing us to and training us in the Care Ministry Network.
>
> — *Pastor Chuck*

A Metropolitan Area

The following report comes from a church in a more metropolitan area:

> I believe in the Care Ministry Network! Our church has experienced a 40 percent growth in attendance since its inception. Much of this growth I attribute to the implementation of this ministry. Our people are getting cared for at a level that we previously were unable to offer them.
>
> The Care Ministry Network has opened up a new avenue of serving for some in the church who have not had the

opportunity before in any other area of ministry. As some people are providing care and others are receiving care, they become more dedicated and become a more integral part of the church body.

I highly recommend Dr. John Bosman and the Care Ministry Network to any church of any size. This ministry is proven and effective. To us, this is not a program; it is a part of our DNA. With this network in motion, we truly are "caring people caring for people."

— Pastor Mike

A Video Report

One of the churches produced some video recordings of the results of their *Care Ministry*. One of the testimonies was from a couple in their church that said they had heard of the *Care Ministry Network* but didn't pay too much attention to it. They were doubtful about whether they would like to give care or even receive care. They held this perspective until a doctor diagnosed the husband with cancer. For some reason, he and his wife had to stay at the hospital in a city quite a distance from their home.

As I watched this DVD, I could see how his eyes filled with tears time and again as his wife patted his hand and he said, *"I had no idea that this is what the Care Ministry Network entailed. Pastor, this is an excellent ministry. Our Care Pastors showed up the very first day I was admitted and came over to see me so many times I cannot even remember. They prayed as people would, who love me."*

With tears now freely flowing down his cheeks, he went on to say, *"I never expected this attitude. Some of the families in our group prepared meals, others brought food, while yet others helped us with our kids. What we experienced goes way beyond description."*

When Calamity Strikes

In another church, a couple who had been members for many years frankly told their Care Pastors that they did not need them and suggested that instead, they spend their time on some other people who may need their attention.

But not too long after that, one of their close family members died unexpectedly. And to everyone's amazement, they did not call the pastor, but remembered their Care Pastors and called them instead. Sometimes, people think they don't need care until they need it.

Pause the Wedding

Another remarkable event occurred in a church where a young girl, let's call her Jenny, fell hopelessly in love with another Christian young man shortly after she graduated from high school. After only a few short weeks of their relationship, Jenny announced their engagement and, to the shock of everyone, also revealed that they were going to get married shortly.

Jenny's parents were some of those who did not think they needed a Care Pastor. They emphatically said they were a happy and stable family, and for all intents and purposes, they were. But now, ever so suddenly, they realized they needed somebody, and being too embarrassed to turn to their pastor, remembered their Care Pastor.

Fortunately, Jenny respected the younger Care Pastor couple and was willing to listen to their advice.

They lovingly pointed out the risks and dangers and helped her understand that neither she nor the young man was ready for such a massive commitment. They also included the young man in the process and offered to help them both through their journey. It worked out marvelously, as the Care Pastors were instrumental in rescuing two lives before it was too late. It was not the pastor, but an equipped couple in the church who had the gift of mercy with the desire of shepherding, who saved them from an impending disaster and a treacherous cliff.

A Church in a Changing Community

I am Jana Meeks. My husband, Randy, and I pastor Lindale Church in Houston, Texas. I am the Care Ministry Director for our church. We began our Care Group Ministry in March of 2015. It has been a HUGE blessing to us and highly successful in connecting the members to the church body. We have sixteen groups of varying sizes and each has their own unique and particular personality. What the members all have in common is a sincere and heartfelt knowledge that they are all loved and necessary to the church and to each other. As pastors, we have seen a vastly improved avenue of information regarding the health and crisis situation in our church. Our people don't fall through the cracks or become lost in the shuffle. Critical information that sometimes eluded us in the past now has a direct and clear path through our Group Leaders. It just works!

When Storm Clouds Gather

During the recent storm, Harvey, much of our city flooded. Many of our members suffered great loss, with some losing all they ever possessed. We implemented the Care Ministry System in our congregation almost *four* years ago. During Harvey, our Care Leaders stayed in touch with their members and kept us, the church leadership, informed as to everyone's condition.

One of our Care Leaders became extremely concerned for one of their families who was stranded while the water kept rising until it was waist deep. This family consisted of an elderly lady, with Alzheimer's, and four other members. There was no way for them to get out, and rescuers did not seem to know they needed help. The Group Leaders kept phone contact with the family and let us know of their plight. We were finally able to reach a Harris County Sheriff friend who got the attention of a rescue team with a boat, and they were plucked out of their flooded home. Their Leaders stayed with them, continued to minister to them, and helped get them into a hotel.

Another Leader on the other side of town was alerted to the fact that one of his families of four was critically stranded in their home. Their cars were already underwater as the water continued to rise in their home. Their Group Leader decided to step in and drove to the scene as close as he could and then waded through the tainted flood water for many blocks to reach his family group. He got there just in time.

He personally carried one of the kids and some belongings, while the dad and mom were then able to carry the other child along with whatever little possessions they could manage. Their house and what was left in it was completely lost, but their lives were spared. Gabe took them home with him, where they stayed with his family until they could get another place to live.

Robert and Millie Gitau will never forget what their Care Leaders did for them. We could go on and on to tell you more about the courageous deeds of our devoted Care Leaders.

— Pastor Jana

IMPLEMENTATION GUIDELINES

1

THE PASTOR CANNOT DO IT ALONE

Introduction

In this fast-paced life we are living, with packed church calendars and overstressed people, pastors often question how they can help their church members personally and truthfully experience the love of God. They realize that many of their people feel overlooked and neglected because they cannot reach all their people as adequately as they desire on their own. Added to this frustration is the fact that in most cases, churches cannot afford to employ enough staff to sufficiently take care of all their members on a regular basis.

Without a practical resolve, more and more people will fall through the cracks and wander away from the church for lack of attention. This, understandably, causes pastors to live in angst and because of the nature of their calling, search for a solution to this ever-growing challenge. There must be an answer to this crying need — and, thank God, there is!

The proven solution is found in a system of care that is designed to enable church members to care for one another in a prescribed way in partnership with their pastor and under the leadership of an appointed director. All people need attention or support at some point in time. When that is not received from their church family, they tend to feel slighted and rejected. This responsibility inevitably becomes overwhelming, especially when a church begins to grow. That's why we must turn to the Biblical solution which lies within equipping the saints for the work of the ministry.

We cannot and should not release people into the ministry role of caring for others without first adequately preparing and training them for this important task. According to Ephesians 4:11-13, pastors, as part of the Five-fold ministry, are responsible for equipping their people for the work of the ministry, which includes caring for one another. That is the primary reason why we have put this handbook together.

Our motive for involving church members in care ministry is not so pastors can hand off the so-called "boring" work to them as they continue with the supposed "real work of ministry". It's a *partnership* that we have in mind — doing ministry together. We hold that all who are Christ's should be involved in ministry and that every believer is, therefore, a minister. We want to reverse the accepted notion that members *help* the pastor in ministry, to the reality of the *pastor being the one that helps the people* to discover, develop, and deploy their gifts.

The care ministry concept we have developed, is not designed to only provide care to people when they face a crisis of some sorts, but to provide care when they are *not* facing hardship. Our dictate is to develop meaningful relationships and build a healthy community among the congregants in the good times as well as the hard times. It's the relationship we build when there are no difficulties that earns us the right to be trusted during the tough times.

People are important to God. He sent His Son, Jesus, to die on a cross and make it possible for sinful man to be reconciled to holy God and become part of His glorious family. If people are that important to God, then it only stands to reason that we should give priority to caring for them in the most effective ways. 1 John 4:11 says, "Dear friends, since God so loved us, we also ought to love one another" (NIV).

We Have an Obligation

After people have been born again and become part of the body of Christ, it becomes the local church's responsibility to disciple, nurture, and care for them. It is absurd to think we can leave people on their own and expect them to grow spiritually and experience the love of God if we are not there to provide the support they need. People can only grow spiritually when they are connected relationally. After people have experienced the love of God, they should then experience the Christ-like love of people. It's the only route to survival.

Many other leaders agree with me that meaningful care is a critical component of growing a church. We can win them by the scores and still lose them by the dozens if we do not have a system to care for them.

> Dr. Mel Steinbron said, "Caring and nurturing follow evangelism in the spiritual order in the same way that nurturing follows the birth of a child in the natural order."

> Pastor Larry Osborne writes, "While many would assume that a church focused on bringing people in the front door would have an advantage when it comes to reaching the lost, that's not necessarily true over the long haul. Churches

that close the back door effectively do so by serving their congregations so well that the people don't want to leave. And happy sheep are incurable word-of-mouth marketers."

Care and connection are key to church growth.

Rich Birch says, "I know it can be stylish to think that as a church leader your job is to simply preach the message, to cast a vision for the future, and to let the people care for the flock. In fact, there's a lot of church leaders out there that resist the idea of being a shepherding type, preferring to carry the mantle of business leader or CEO. **What we see in growing churches, however, is a combination of compelling vision and excellent communication with a deep sense of care and connection to the community.**

Growing churches have a robust system for not only getting people connected to the church but also caring for people while they're with the church. Your church may see flash-in-the-pan growth, but you won't be able to sustain that long-term without investing a certain amount of care. If you reach people with a wide variety of needs, you'll need to build a system to figure out how to care for and love those people. **The church is a body caring for each other, not merely an entertaining show or a large non-profit organization.**"[2]

---

[2] 7 Facts About Church Growth That Will Make You Think Twice by Rich Birch as referenced in The Top 10 Leadership Posts I Read the Week of January 7th, by Brian Dodd on Leadership, January 11, 2019. (Unseminary.com)

Until very recently, church members have been reluctant to be involved in ministry, and for many reasons. Today, there is a visible change in the air. People are once again becoming eager to take up their responsibility to be involved in ministry and are seeking opportunities to do so. This attitude change is brought about by the Holy Spirit, creating what some scholars refer to as *The Day of the Saints.*

There is a certain freshness that comes with involving church members in ministry. They come with a different perspective than we who have been in vocational ministry for a long time. They don't see problems the way we do; what we regard as obstacles they often see as opportunities. There is more to developing our people than it just being our responsibility; there is also great joy that comes from doing so. In heaven one day, we are not so much going to be rewarded for the things we have done, but for the people we have developed. If you want to know how to grow a church, grow the people.

Life-giving Churches

We are facing new challenges every day and are confronted with issues we have never faced before around every turn. A good example is the explosion of social media. We find ourselves more connected than ever before, but have in spite of it, become increasingly more reclusive and more distant from each other. This seclusion is not helping us grow healthy churches. God did not create us to live that way. We were shaped for community.

> "Isolating yourself from community is one way to not guard your heart. You need more eyes than your own to help you walk right."
>
> — Jackie Hill Perry

The most obvious place to build wholesome relationships is within the Church. That is our mission. But for us to accomplish this, it will require more than just being friendly to each other on a Sunday or shaking hands with people during fellowship time. We should instead develop purposeful care to all who relate to the congregation. The evident solution is to instill a verified system in our churches whereby we can train church members to come alongside their pastor to provide the required care to each of our church members. I refer to this process as *A Proven New Paradigm for Congregational Care,* which is already functioning in scores of churches.

Just today I received an email from a pastor of a life-giving church in which he said,

> "The Care Ministry Network has been a tremendous blessing to (our church) in numerous ways. It has given us a plan and a strategy that allows us to have ongoing and long-term care to every member of our congregation.
>
> Also, it has given each Care Pastor a great sense of responsibility and ownership as they help to tend the flock, not to mention it has helped the congregation to feel loved and truly cared for.
>
> The Care Ministry Network has taken a huge burden off the shoulders of the staff knowing that each member is receiving more than just crisis care. This is a tool that every church needs to implement."

When members are trained and involved in caring for one another, the pastors quickly sense unbelievable freedom from the pressure of trying to meet the needs of all the people all the time. Their appreciation and gratitude towards their people become visible as both pastors and church members alike understand the principle that all who are Christ's have a responsibility to build His Church. Many believers clearly have some of the essential virtues that qualify them to ably care for others: understanding, kindheartedness, realness, readiness, dependability, caring attitude, attentiveness, availability, and the ability to encourage. The truth is that it does not require a professional to love people, all you need is a heart for people, and a willingness to be there for them.

> "Every human being has a great, yet often unknown, gift to care, to be compassionate, to become present to the other, to listen, to hear and to receive. If that gift would be set free and made available, miracles could take place. Those who can sit in silence with their fellow man not knowing what to say, but knowing that they should be there, can bring new life in a dying heart. Those who are not afraid to hold a hand in gratitude, to shed tears in grief, and to let a sign of distress arise straight from the heart, can break through paralyzing boundaries and witness the birth of a new fellowship" (The late Henri Nouwen).

Church Members Have the Capacity

As astounding as it may sound to some, it's true that church members can effectively provide congregational care if they are trained, developed, and given the opportunity. We rob many wonderful people of their Spirit-given gifts and kill ourselves in the process by trying to handle pastoral care at the expense of our congregants. I really appreciate the way Dr. Alastair Campbell states his viewpoint of providing care:

> "Pastoral care ... is not correctly understood if it is viewed within the framework of professionalism ... Pastoral care is a relationship founded upon the integrity of the individual. Such a relationship does not depend primarily upon the acquisition of knowledge or the development of skill. Rather, it depends upon a caring attitude toward others, which comes from our own experience of pain, fears, and loss, and our own release from their deadening grip"[3]

Dr. Campbell continues this thought and refers to those caring for others as *enfleshed love.* That may most likely be the best way to describe our people involved in caring for others. The following story illustrates this point very well:

> "'Mommy, Mommy, I'm afraid,' cried the little girl who was awakened in the middle of the night by the storm. The rain beating against the window frightened her; the lightning and thunder terrified her. 'Mommy, where are you! Where are you?'
>
> "Her mother hurried into her room. She sat on the side of the bed and held her daughter tightly to comfort her. Wanting to take advantage of this teachable moment, she said, 'Honey,

---

3   (Alastair Campbell, *Rediscovering Pastoral Care* (Philadelphia, PA: Westminster Press, 1981), p. 41).

when you are frightened like this you can know that God is with you and He loves you.'

"'Yes, Mommy, I know that,' she sobbed. 'But I need love with skin on!'"[4]

If there has ever been a clear definition of the Care Ministry Network, then it is: *"Being love with skin on!"* There are moments in our lives when we just need someone to *be* there — someone to show up — someone to be love with skin on.

Mary Humphries, who with her husband, Ric, joined our staff at Glad Tidings Church in 1987, still does most of the proofreading of my books — even though neither of us are at the church any longer. I recently sent her one of the chapters to edit. After she had worked through the chapter, she responded by telling me how much the contents blessed her and stirred her to send me the following account:

> "The emphasis on understanding that we have to take care of our people so they can be healthy enough to serve and minister to others is a lesson everyone in the church world needs to learn. It's so easy to take people for granted and even wonder why they aren't doing more, when we really need to let them know they are valued and appreciated. And, sometimes all it takes is a little heartfelt pastoral care — a phone call to say, "I notice you were missing," an email saying, "I prayed for you today," showing up to celebrate a

---

[4]   (Steinbron, Melvin J, *Can the Pastor do it Alone,* Wipf & Stock Publishers, Eugene, OR 97401. Pg. 25. Used with permission.)

birthday with them or to share a sorrow. I have a friend here who has been teaching me the importance of "showing up." I may feel too tired that day, or maybe I don't think it will matter to others, or it just doesn't seem that important — but it is important to just "show up." I don't have to bring a gift, words of wisdom, or even the answer to their problem. I just need to show up and let them know *they matter to me!"*

Caring for others is not complicated or difficult. The basic requirement is simply to have the gift of mercy (which so many believers have), a passion for others, and the willingness to be available. Receiving training in how to systematically approach people and maintain an ongoing relationship will take you a long way in being effective.

Humankind Was Created for Community
God never had a solitary lifestyle in mind for His followers. His idea of us being part of a family describes the way He intended for us to live in community with each other. As Rick Warren says, ". . . we are fashioned for fellowship, and formed for a family, and none of us can fulfill God's purposes by ourselves. The Bible knows nothing of solitary saints or spiritual hermits."

When we withdraw from people and isolate ourselves from our friends it is usually because of our own choices, life circumstances, and personal hurt and pain. Separating from friends during the crucial experiences in life is the worst decision any person can ever make. Even Jesus, in His greatest moment of sorrow in the Garden of Gethsemane, needed Peter, James, and John (His friends) to be nearby during the greatest agony of His life.

"Then Jesus went with them to a garden called Gethsemane and told his disciples, 'Stay here while I go over there and pray.' Taking along Peter and the two sons of Zebedee, he plunged into an agonizing sorrow. Then he said, 'This sorrow is crushing my life out. Stay here and keep vigil with me'" (Matthew 26:36-38 MSG).

Humankind was created for companionship and humans feel deprived when they are left to themselves. People today are in search of opportunities to build relationships and develop friendships. "They are not necessarily looking for a friendly church; it's friends they are after." There are multiple friendly churches to be found everywhere, but there are not that many churches that are intentionally developing practical ways for people to connect and stay connected. The obvious key to help people connect is through establishing a system of ongoing care to each member in the congregation. In our genre of care, we emphatically state that we do not care for people only in crisis times, but at all times.

Christ-like Relationships

We belong to God's family, the Body of Christ, and, as such, should be connected to every other member. The Bible says, "In Christ we who are many, form one body, and each member belongs to all the others" (Romans 12:5 NIV). Rick Warren goes on to say, "While your relationship with Christ is personal, God never intends it to be private. In God's family, you are connected to every other believer."

God has divinely created us to be shaped and formed through other believers, and that we in return should shape and form others. Developing relationships with other people is simply a natural inclination within mankind, and is, beside seeking salvation, one of the main reasons why people even come to our churches.

When people who join a church do not closely connect with at least six other people within six months, they are likely to quietly slip away again. Losing members is undoubtedly one of the greatest heartaches of any pastor. They cannot help but take it personally. It is not merely the loss of members that troubles us, but, more importantly, the deprivation of the opportunity to help them go through the discipleship process and become part of the full functioning of the body of Christ. One of the proven ways we can sustain the growth of a church is by ensuring that we have ways and means of developing and growing our people spiritually. In the process, we guide them to be integrated in the community of the congregation.

It's the culture we cultivate that matters, not only a concept we implement. It's not so much what we *do*, but who we *are* as a congregation that makes the impact. People may initially be attracted to a church because of something that caught their attention, but once in, they quickly become aware of the church politics, cliques, and relational dysfunction that is deeply imbedded in the congregation. People then usually don't stay, but rather opt out for a more genuine, loving church where people truly care and are serious about the matter.

> **It's not only about the new believers.**

Not only new members, but also our established church members require loving care in a consistent way. This is what makes them feel accepted and valued. They are the ones we should protect and support. They are the people who faithfully undergird the congregation and are the viable candidates who should be equipped for the work of the ministry. We dare not neglect them. People are our greatest assets and the only instruments the Lord has chosen to help Him build His Church. It's through them, and only them, that we can fulfill the local church's mission. We make a big mistake if we constantly concentrate only on the new people coming in at the neglect of the sheep God had already given us. If we don't take care of the people God has already given us, why should He send us more?

> We need all the people of God, to do all the work of God. [Mel Steinbron]

In our concept of care, we do not seek to simply keep people after we reap them, but instead, spiritually grow them to become healthy enough to go out and bring in the sheaves. Our goal, therefore, is not to see how large we can grow a congregation, but to see how healthy we can make it become. When we feed the sheep and care for them, nature teaches us, they will produce the lambs and secure the succession. A church is set for stimulating growth only when the members are cared for and are healthy — to the point where discipleship becomes the natural outflow of passionate and motivated people. A sick church simply cannot do that; at least not effectively.

Caring People, Caring for People

In *Care Revolution*, I discuss the basic human needs all people have under the chapter heading, "Why People Act the Way They Do". We have learned that all humankind has five basic needs that do not change geographically, genetically, or even culturally. We will greatly miss the goal if we assume that we should only take care of the spiritual needs of people at the neglect of the basic human needs they have.[5]

In Search of Understanding

Since the message of Christ is a message of love, acceptance, and forgiveness, many people come to our congregations expecting to find understanding, protection, and genuine care. Scores of hurting people make their way to our churches, desperately seeking healing and compassion. Oftentimes, they do not only seek forgiveness of their sin but genuine support to break free from the shackles of shame that are keeping them bound.

It is only in an environment of love and acceptance that they feel secure, which results in them feeling comfortable enough to trust people and thus become willing to let go of their bondages of the past. This attitude becomes the stimulus that gives hurting people the courage and will to want to become whole again and simultaneously encourages them to earnestly seek meaningful purpose in life once more. We want to develop churches to become *that kind of church* to a hurting world — caring people, caring for people — being the presence of Christ in our communities. But we also understand that it not only calls for a vision change, it calls for a culture change. We have to create an atmosphere of genuine care by means of love, acceptance, and forgiveness. We should reach out to people who are facing tough times and have them

---

[5] We will not discuss the details of human necessities here again but recommend that you take some time to read the contents of what I deliberated on the subject in *The Care Revolution*. It will help you immensely to gain insight into the behavior of people.

experience the love of Christ through a caring body of believers. We must become the change agents in a hurting world.

R.T. Kendall in his daily devotion "By Love Transformed" in *Charisma* magazine, (02/23/2013) echoes this viewpoint when he writes:

> "'I have loved you,' says the Lord. —Malachi 1:2
>
> Victor Hugo, the nineteenth-century French writer, said, 'The supreme happiness in life is the conviction that we are loved.
>
> "We all have a need to be loved. When people are difficult to understand, when I wonder what makes them tick, I find that what they most need, and what they most want, is to be loved. There is nothing that breaks the hardest heart like the feeling of being loved. All of us can face terrible opposition and suffering if we feel approved, accepted, and loved by someone whose opinion matters to us.
>
> "There is an even greater feeling than knowing another person loves you, and that is knowing that God loves you. There is no greater feeling than that. When I feel that God loves me and approves of me, I can face a thousand foes. And the message of Malachi is just that, 'You are loved.' We all have skeletons in our closets, and God knows every one of them, yet He still says, 'I love you.'"[6]

---

[6] Excerpted from Between the Times (Christian Focus Publications Ltd., 2003).

The Love of God and the Love of People

Momentous restoration in people's lives is most effective when both the love of God and the love of people are felt. God makes forgiveness, grace, and mercy available, and people provide acceptance, safety, and security. We should sincerely ask ourselves if we are intentionally doing all we can to minister love to those God has entrusted to us. Do our people genuinely feel loved? Do they feel accepted? Do they truly experience a sense of belonging? Are they connected relationally? And the bigger question is, does this love flow out to the streets of our communities?

The purpose of the *Care Ministry Network* is to cultivate a *culture of care* that will permeate the entire congregation without making it become ingrown or self-centered. A dysfunctional church family simply cannot accomplish its God-given task and be effective *witnesses for Christ in Jerusalem, and in all Judea and Samaria, and to the end of the earth* (Acts 1:8b).

Our Focus

Our focus for instilling a care ministry is three-fold. *First*, we want to decrease the load the pastor carries concerning congregational care. *Second*, we want to make room for believers to be involved in actual work of the ministry. *Third*, we desire to provide authentic and constant care to each member in the congregation that results in spiritual and emotional health.

The pastor casts the vision, trains the people, and then launches the ministry. We have team ministry in mind where definite roles and expectations are set. In the process church members do not *replace* the pastor, they *represent* their pastor. Preparing people for ministry can only effectively be done by utilizing proven curriculum and outlines that follow a prescribed design. These are all readily available on our website.

We already know the present-day way of providing care to a congregation is not working. We need a totally new perspective that, in many ways, may require a paradigm shift that will change our thinking, attitudes, and perspective regarding people involvement in ministry.

> Dr. Jim Garlow says, *"The contagious churches of the next century will be different from traditional churches today. One revolutionary difference will revolve around pastoral care. The exciting prospect is that everyone in the congregation will receive regular pastoral care from a gifted and trained layperson."*[7]

This assertion Dr. Garlow makes defines aptly what the answer is to the question of our day for providing overall congregational care — member involvement. Many churches will be healthier and more poised for growth when we change the way we provide pastoral care. This may certainly require us to change our focus regarding the ways we have been prioritizing ministry.

Winning the lost should always be our rudimentary mission; we can never stop reaching out to a dying world. We have never questioned that responsibility. What we have neglected is creating the corresponding obligation to integrate those Christ entrusts to us into our care. We applaud new converts when they make a decision for Christ but leave them on the sidewalks of life without help after their leap of faith.

---

7   Endorsement of the *Care Revolution* on back cover.

We have a responsibility to care about those who are drawn to our churches, as well as those who have been part of the family for an extended time. Without sensible *in-reach* we will never have effective *outreach*. Through the *Care Revolution* we are driven to see churches revitalized through the Christ kind of love at work in us to reach the unreached segments of our communities. Our mission is to be a force of revolution in a desperate, hurting, and dying world. We are the light, and light never flees from darkness — darkness bolts when the light shows up. For us to become effective light-bearers, we must make an effort to identify the pain of society around us and find ways and means to make a difference. But, allow me to say it again: The love of God has to flow down the aisles of our churches before it will flow down the streets of our cities.

> The love of God should flow down the aisles of our churches before it will flow down the streets of our cities!

Atmosphere

Cultivating a *culture of care* requires us to create the desired atmosphere in our churches. *Atmosphere* is important because we have learnt that some things grow vigorously in a certain atmosphere, while other things die in the same atmosphere. When we create an atmosphere of love, acceptance, and forgiveness — peace, tranquility, and joy grow. At the same time, dissension, strife, tension, and gossip die. To create this kind of atmosphere requires Christ-like love, unpretentious concern, and genuine acceptance.

Atmosphere is crucial in a church: Before large numbers of new babes are born into the Kingdom, God first seeks for a church with the warmest atmosphere of love and care He can find. When a congregation has developed such an environment, God will continually bless that church with new believers. That's why effective congregational care is so vital.

Our Purpose Should be Calculated

Simply preaching on the subject or encouraging people to love one another in a Biblical fashion alone will not solve the problem. It may quite possibly just evoke more guilt and make the climate more negative and stressed. If people do not know *how* to care, then *why* they should care really doesn't matter. If loving doesn't translate into caring, it will make no difference. Caring for people should be the delight of the entire congregation.

In his book, *Everyone a Minister*, Oscar Feucht aptly says it like this: "An adequate ministry is not a one-man ministry. It is not even a corps of associated pastors. It is the whole church, congregation-by-congregation, mobilized and trained for mission. Only this strategy is adequate."[8]

The greatest disaster that ever came to the Church was when the ministry was moved from the *people* to the *professionals* and from the *pew* to the *pulpit*. During the First Reformation, the Church gave the *Bible* back to the people, and now, in the present milieu, the Church is giving the *ministry* back to the people. It's the day of the Saints and every believer is a minister!

---

8 (Oscar E. Feucht, Everyone A Minister (Philadelphia: Westminster Press, 1974) p.80.

"Christianity has become nothing but a spectator sport. It looks very much like a football game with 22 men on the field desperately in need of rest, and twenty-two thousand in the grandstands, desperately in need of exercise." (Ray C. Stedman)

One of the main reasons why churches decline in numbers is because, for the greater part, people have become bored and feel left out. The most effective way of getting a church off a plateau is by getting people to participate in ministry. The *Care Ministry* has proven to be an energetic catalyst in getting large numbers of people involved very quickly.

> They that row
> the boat,
> don't have
> time to rock it!

The Handbook

The *Handbook* is specifically designed to help navigate members of a local church through the unfamiliar territory of launching a congregational care system. The success of the voyage is determined by involving church members to come on board not to be passengers on a cruise ship, but soldiers on a battleship. These are ordinary men and women who serve in partnership with their pastor, who come alongside their fellow congregants to ensure that no one falls through the cracks or struggles on their own.

> Our goal is to raise an army
> not just an audience!

Preparing for the Launch

The launching stage of the *Care Ministry Network* is crucial, and the more time you spend on laying a firm foundation, the stronger the framework of the ministry will be. Since the *Care Ministry Network* is an unfamiliar concept to many, and since I provide so much information in this handbook, it's only logical that all leaders, along with *all members-in-training*, should each have their personal copy. Having this material in-hand makes it so much easier for all involved to more fully grasp the stages of launching and especially maintaining a healthy care network.

Christ Has No Body
Christ has no body but yours,
No hands, no feet on earth but yours,
Yours are the eyes with which He looks
Compassion on this world,
Yours are the feet with which He walks to do good,
Yours are the hands, with which He blesses all the world.
Yours are the hands, yours are the feet,
Yours are the eyes, you are His body.

— *Teresa of Arvila*

2

THE ESSENCE OF CONGREGATIONAL CARE

The *Care Ministry* concept is not a means of creating a professional platform that requires specific educational or credentialed levels. It is rather a means of utilizing the gifts of men and women who already have the basic qualifications given to them by the Holy Spirit.

Our challenge has never really been the lack of capable people, but instead the erroneous belief that pastoral care belongs exclusively to the pastor. That is the mindset we need to change. We are overlooking the valuable resources God has given us and continue to see pastors burn out and fail because of the stress and strain. When we do not utilize the gifts of our people, they become highly frustrated and many times leave the church in search of ministry opportunities elsewhere. As the saying goes: If you don't use them, you will lose them!

CYCLE OF MINISTRY

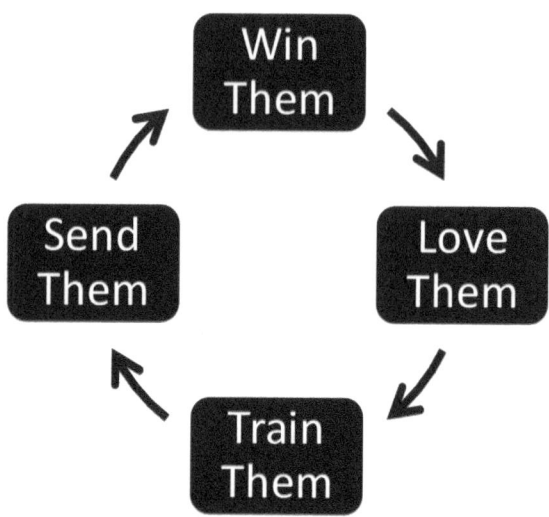

Care Flows from the Heart of the Pastor

The Lead Pastor must be absolutely comfortable with the idea of embracing church members to partner with him or her to provide congregational care or else it will never succeed. It is their enthusiasm and support that gives vitality to this ministry and provides the stability to sustain the concept. This ministry, like all others, should always be the extension of the Lead Pastor's vision.

To be sure, the motivation for launching a care ministry should never be to simply fill ministry slots, keep people involved, pacify lonely people, or to create another program. *Caring for the Flock* should always be the incentive. Our goal is to make sure that all people experience *community*, feel accepted, and know that they belong. From the lead pastor to every member, we desire to create a loving and functional family that is healthy enough to accept others into their embrace.

After having said all that, I want to help set some pastors free. It may sound very strange at the outset but is very true, nevertheless. There are many pastors who do not have *caring* as their dominant gift. And that's okay. The strength of their giftedness may lie in other areas, such as leadership, preaching, teaching, visioneering, administration, etc. That certainly does not make them *bad* pastors, and certainly does not mean they do not care about their people. It only defines who they are, and even more so, which gifts they have received. Some of the greatest pastors in America today readily admit that their giftedness lies in areas other than *pastoring* or *caring* and we have to recognize it.

One such pastor related it to me in a very practical and understandable way when he said, "As a pastor, I love my people. I really do. I have always wanted what's best for them. My gifting lies within teaching and I love to spend hours in preparation to feed the sheep. That's the way I believe I take care of God's people." The packed bookshelves attest to the fact that teaching is where his heart is. There were rows and rows of commentaries, encyclopedias, book sets, and numerous books on all kinds of subjects. Even looking at the media he had installed will let you know that this man loves to study. "But when my secretary reminds me to attend to someone in the hospital," he continued, "I often feel tempted to send an associate. I feel as though I am betraying my calling when I must get up and leave. Studying is where I want to be."

And I know this man very well. He sincerely cares about his people. He will protect them with everything in his might. He believes the best way to serve his people is by preparing well. And he is certainly not wrong. "But strange as it may seem, once I get there," he explained, "I enjoy every moment of being with whoever is in the hospital. I love on them, talk, visit, laugh, pray, and very often even cry with them. If they are seriously ill, I'll stay with them through the night. But when I head back to my office, I sense the excitement rising as I ponder the subject matter of what I am studying."

Does that make him a bad pastor? Absolutely not! His gifting lies more in teaching than pastoring, but you can look at his people: They are spiritually very healthy, and the church is doing exceptionally well. What he needed was a care ministry to bring balance to the congregation. Pastors who do not fall into the category of caring should be cautious to not step into the trap of disregarding this ministry concept simply because it does not resonate with the grace zone of their calling.

Those pastors, on the other hand, who have a true calling of being shepherds and have a passion for *caring,* will typically and spontaneously gravitate towards a concept such as this care ministry network. It is their heart. They care for their people affectionately and in many cases would rather be with the people than be locked up in an office, preparing and studying. Does that make these pastors bad pastors? Again, absolutely not! Hospital visits energize them, it doesn't drain them. What is true, however, is that there should be healthy balance. They, on the other hand, should be careful to not neglect evangelism, discipleship, and teaching. They can so love the sheep that they don't spend time in reaching the lost or growing their people spiritually.

Care? What Do We Mean by Care?

After having spoken to scores of pastors across the country, I have come to realize that most churches are not really providing *pastoral care,* as they suppose. As I have said in the *Care Revolution*: they are in fact only providing *crisis care.* It is only when members face some form of crisis that the pastor shows up. But the honest truth is that with the schedules pastors face today, they can hardly do any more than handle crisis moments.

The new normal we have been forced to live with has made us respond mainly when someone's in the hospital, or very ill at home, or death has occurred, or there is a marriage or family crisis, or even a financial or food crisis, etc. Then, care is aptly provided. But in most cases, when the crisis is over, so is the care. But what about the many other people who face no crisis; should they not also receive attention? Must they wait until they too face the storms of life before someone will show up? When we refer to congregational care through the *Care Ministry Network,* we mean providing comprehensive care to all our members at all times, not only during crisis moments.

Finding the People

The question may very well arise: But where do we find the people? The truth is that we already have all the people we need sitting in our pews every Sunday. We, for the most part, just don't know about them, and the reason for this is because we have never created a ministry model that meets the needs of their giftedness. Once we create such a platform, they come to light. We have found that there are few other ministries that get so many people involved so rapidly as with the *Care Ministry Network.*

When identifying people, be careful to not specifically seek only for those who may fit the profile of what you may consider to be a *professional* minister. Instead, be on the lookout for spiritual gifts and abilities more than appearances. We need to have faith enough in the Lord to help us identify people according to the gifts He has given them and not according to the manmade expectations we have set.

In your selection process, also be careful to not relegate this ministry to seniors only. I am specifically mentioning this, because I have often heard pastors say something like, "Oh yes, we have a good group of seniors in our church that would love to run this ministry." I like that thought. Some of the most effective Care Pastors in our church were retired couples, so that's not the point. One such couple came to me one day and said, "Pastor, we love people and we have a lot of time on our hands. May we please have ten families to take care of? And if some of the other Care Pastors get busy, we can help them too." Troy and Joy did a phenomenal job! They gave their lives to caring for people.

If we create the impression that we are targeting only seniors to be involved in the ministry of care, we will lose the goal we have of reaching the entire congregation. It would not be advisable on the other hand to major on younger people exclusively, either. The most effective way of building your team of care ministers is to have a well-balanced age spread that completely represents the demographics of your church.

Now, let's consider some other important elements of selecting people:

First, there are those who are like low hanging fruit you can easily identify as having the exact fit for this specific ministry. These are the obvious people to be personally invited by the pastor. Never assume they will automatically respond on their own. Sometimes people, even if they have the giftedness, do not in their own minds always feel qualified enough to care for others. Remember, most people still have the notion that pastoral care should exclusively be done by the vocational pastors. If they have what you think is needed, invite them to attend the training conference. Their pastor's confidence in them may be all they will need to make themselves available.

Second, there are likely some who already know their calling, have been waiting for this opportunity, and would jump at a newly created ministry. You certainly want these folks to be part of your care ministry who may even help in the initial stages of the launch. Caution: Some people who are already, on their own volition, providing care to others in some fashion, may feel that they do not need any training or development. You should never, for many reasons, agree to have them skip your training conference.

Third, there are often people who have been involved in a similar ministry in another church and would eagerly desire to be part of the care ministry you are about to launch. These people could potentially be very helpful, but do not consider having them skip the training conference either. As a matter of fact, if they are emphatic, they do not want to undergo the training, you have to be very cautious. It may very well be a red flag. You simply do not want to involve people with an unteachable spirit. Regardless of people's ministry background, one of our goals for the training conference is to ensure that everyone is on the same page and following the same pattern so equal ministry can be provided across the board. The care concept we propose is designed with a deliberate plan of action in mind and if not equivalently applied by everyone can cause unnecessary confusion.

Be All Inclusive

When you begin to cast the vision of your care ministry, make sure your people fully understand that this ministry opportunity is being made available to all members of the congregation. Do not concentrate only on the those you think may qualify, or those that respond first. If you would do so, I can assure you, you are going to overlook someone who is very capable and most eager to serve but does not have the initial courage to make themselves available. If not included, these folks will experience unbelievable rejection. A once cooperative member can then potentially turn into a disgruntled and unsettled person. Their immediate reaction is usually the feeling of not being good enough. Always keep the door open for those the Great Shepherd may want to invite.

The best advice I can give you is to invite everyone to attend the training conference. Once they have been exposed to the full spectrum of the ministry, people who do not have the calling or desire to fulfill the expected obligations, drop out on their own accord.

Follow These Easy Steps
- Cast the vision to the entire congregation in a series of teachings over three or four weekends.
- Explain the concept of congregational care as clearly as possible, based on Scriptural values.
- Take time to clarify the new paradigm of care which allows church members to provide care to one another.
- Make sure everyone understands that significant training will be provided, and that no one will be left on their own.
- At the end of the series, invite *all* members to enroll in the training conference

Not all who attend the training conference will become care pastors, but the more people are informed, the easier it will be to implement the ministry.

This Is How It Gets Done

Church members are not developed to serve in miniature roles of that of the Lead Pastor, they perform actual duties of passion and care. They are not expected to preach, teach, conduct meetings, prepare weekly lessons, or do counseling. They do not have to possess in-depth knowledge of the Bible or have some form of ministry credentials. Since they will not be teaching a group of people, the ability to teach is not a qualification either. If they can love people, they can care for people.

Developing members to become care pastors is fulfilling the New Testament principle of all believers being ministers. If they are ably equipped (which is more than just a classroom experience), the care they give, can be equivalent to that of the vocational staff, if not surpassed. It is for this reason that the *Care Ministry Network* attempts to bring in-depth training and teaching, which goes beyond simplistic notes and head knowledge.

When care pastors are actively involved in praying, visiting, nurturing, encouraging, and caring for their fellow church members, pastors will tell you that the overwhelming blessing to them means freedom, sincere gratitude, deep satisfaction, peaceful sleep, and the joy of knowing that shared ministry brings strength and blessing to God's people.

> The Church should not run on the feet of the clergy, but on the feet of the laity.

Some Crucial First Steps

There are four cardinal factors you should take into consideration as you prepare for launching your Care Ministry. Circumventing these simple-but-crucial four foundational blocks may result in your care ministry to not be as effective as you had hoped.

Here are the four essential steps that will help you lay a strong foundation:
1. Congregational Care should be **planned**.
2. Congregational Care must be **intentional**.
3. Congregational Care must be **structured**.
4. Congregational Care should be **available to everyone**.

1. Congregational Care Should Be Planned (Acts 6:1-7)

One of the greatest mistakes a pastor can make in starting a care ministry is to not spend adequate time planning and strategizing the process of this ministry. If it is done in a haphazard way, people will never take it seriously and likewise not buy into it either. Just as we plan other parts of our church such as education, evangelism, worship, finances, and properties, we must also plan for the care of our membership.

> Dr. Kenneth Haugk writes: ". . . a caring ministry requires the same thoughtful planning as other dimensions of congregational life. In fact, planning for caring should receive special attention, because the congregation's call to care for people in times of hurt or need or crisis is at the very heart of a congregation's existence and life."[9]

---

9   (Stephen Series Newsletter, Summer 1985, Stephen Ministries, 8016 Dale Avenue, St Louis, MO 63117)

Most of the things we are talking about here fall within the category of *normal* for any organization but need to be lifted out so as to not make light of putting the ministry together. Planning congregational care means there is a defined process to be considered and the following should be well-thought-out:[10]

- Gatherings to be scheduled
- Deadlines to meet
- People to be involved
- Budgets to consider
- Facility resources to contemplate
- Personnel to be involved
- And the list continues

In your planning, it's important to place the functions of the care ministry in the church calendar and make room for its activities. It cannot and should not be left to happen in a nonchalant way with no organization built into it. Never take on the idea of *we will plan it as we go along*.

Those events you place in the church calendar are aimed mostly at those involved in care ministry and does not necessarily affect the whole membership. It's important to be aware of this, because if we're not careful, it may seem as though a single ministry has taken over the entire church.

---

10 (I want to be careful that you do not get the impressions that these are hard and fast rules that make everything complicated. I have instead penned these points as helpful thought-provokers in your preparation, so you don't miss anything.)

2. Congregational Care Must Be Intentional

Care will never happen by itself — even in a church setting where people are friendly and kind and pray together. There should be an intentional effort to implement a system through which functional care could be achieved. *Intentionality* is the key to the effectiveness of the care ministry and is the most overlooked element in many of our ministries — especially as it relates to care and community. Members have to be trained to *intentionally* reach out to others.

Many times, when I address the need for intentional *care* in a church, I often hear people say, "We already have a loving and caring congregation; we don't need a specific care ministry." And, for the most part, they are correct. They laugh, talk, hug, pray, and even support each other in the church foyer, and sometimes even in the aisles. There is clearly a bond of love when they come together, no doubt. But these actions don't translate into genuine care for others. It does not build community and ends up a fellowship, at best.

There is a huge difference between fellowship and ongoing congregational care. Our relationships generally fall into a ditch when the final *amen* is said and each of us go our own way. Very few people are concerned about what happens in the lives of their fellow believers and, except for some of their personal friends, aren't even in touch with any others during the week.

The unfortunate truth is that people often leave our services with the same hurts they came with because nobody cared. When people drive off, all go their own way, and everyone is pretty much left to themselves. Those who are facing no challenges, or demands, go on with their lives and live life to its fullest. Those who have some serious challenges, however, arrive back home, disillusioned, because they had hoped their needs would be met, or that someone would have reached out to them in their valley, but no one did.

Until we *intentionally* begin to reach out to other people and show specific acts of compassionate kindness it will remain an expectation and never an expression of genuine care. Said in another way: Care doesn't happen by accident; it happens on purpose. If we desire to see the fruit of adequate congregational care, we must know that it begins with the seed of intentionality.

> **Care doesn't happen by accident; it happens on purpose.**

Unless congregational care becomes intentional, the fundamental ministry of caring simply will not happen, despite a generally accepted, loving church family. Those who do not have a high profile in the congregation are usually the ones who fall through the cracks and many times slip through the back door. They are, unfortunately, not quickly missed and tend to finally drift away from the church. Many times, these folks are jewels that could have been very instrumental in the church. And let's face it, they are the ones that fill the seats on Sunday. That is often the reason why we see new faces in the crowd but never see the attendance chart go upward.

Intentionality may very well be what Jesus had in mind when He gave us the parable of the lost sheep. The moral of this story is: "Watch that you don't treat a single one of these childlike believers arrogantly . . . Look at it this way. If someone has a hundred sheep and one of them wanders off, doesn't he leave the ninety-nine and go after the one? And if he finds it, doesn't he make far more over it than over the ninety-nine who stay put? Your Father in heaven feels the same way.

He doesn't want to lose even one of these simple believers" (Matthew 18:10-14 MSG).

This parable describes a scenario of a sheep that went astray. We many times use this parable to explain the importance of evangelism, and that's fine. But within its context it refers to a sheep that had already been counted as part of the flock that had wandered off — a member of the household of faith, not a stranger in the world. The shepherd was concerned about a sheep not a goat ("outsider"). It seems as though Jesus, in this parable, is teaching us the important lesson of valuing each member of the flock and showing us by illustration the necessity of caring about people intentionally.

Care should never be assumed to *just happen*. As a matter of fact, it never will. Not even when we faithfully preach about loving one another. This is exactly where most churches are missing the key component of growing their churches and developing a healthy body of believers. Congregational care should be *intentional*. Period. That is the only way we can live out the Biblical statement of "*if one member suffers, the whole body suffers . . .*" Each member should *intentionally* (with purpose) be connected to someone else.

3. Congregational Care Should Be Structured

Just as all the other ministries in the church are programmed, calculated, and organized, the ministry of congregational care should likewise be well-planned and *structured*. There should be levels of leadership, lines of authority, and avenues of communication, with designated roles and responsibilities assigned to people. Without a deliberate, though simple, structure, this ministry will not be effective. It will be destined to mediocrity at best and failure at worst. When a ministry is organized it just makes it so much easier to operate.

Exodus 18: 13–26 provides a good example for us to follow in developing structure in ministry. I cover more of this in depth in the *Care Revolution*. Moses activated a practical organizational structure, which proved to be successful and simultaneously assured his own survival. It is clear that the mission would have failed if he had not developed a sensible structure through which everyone could operate.[11]

Any pastor and church can learn from the advice Jethro gave Moses to develop an efficient organizational structure for ministry. God has entrusted us with the responsibility of developing people spiritually and involving them personally. Developing ministry requires an understanding of how to systematize our churches and how to connect people with each other in a sensible way.

4. Congregational Care Should Be Provided to Everyone

For too long, many individuals in our churches have felt neglected as they see others receiving attention over and over. The premise of the *Care Ministry Network* is to provide care to all members in a simple, yet effective, way.

The important aspect of this statement is that care should not only be provided to the congregants, but also to those in leadership. It is senseless to not provide care to those who are providing the care. They too have challenges to face and struggles to deal with in life. We cannot afford to have them ever function in a vacuum and never have anyone to also check on their well-being and celebrate with them at joyous occasions.

Providing care for all should even include the Lead Pastor. They will tell you that they preach to large numbers on Sunday and pray

---

11   See illustrations in the *Care Revolution*, pages 333-4.

with scores of people, but when they drive off, they feel lonely and wished that there was someone who would reach out to them also. Someone needs to reach out to the pastor and his/her family.

All people face challenges at some point

Although some may not admit it initially, everyone will at some point face a challenge in their lives and will appreciate someone being there for them. We are not created to live on our own. We are created for community. When storm clouds gather, all people have a propensity to grasp onto someone for help. Sometimes these needs will be obvious — such as sickness, a threatening divorce, financial burdens, broken relationships, a wayward child, death, etc. At times needs may not necessarily be visible — such as emotions, fear, mid-life crisis, loneliness, starvation for love, forgiveness, and the list continues.

Then again, people may have challenges that relate to their future — aging, pending death of a loved one, career or job change, retirement, diagnosis of a doctor, outcome of a court case, or some other challenges. At other times people may have spiritual needs — such as discipleship, prayer, Biblical questions, assurance of salvation, and more. Helping people to find spiritual direction is certainly part of pastoral care. Care Pastors are not expected to disciple people in-depth or to teach them Biblical truths, but they should be knowledgeable regarding the church's spiritual growth tracks.

Once trained, sincere and observant Care Pastors will find multitudes of occasions to serve their people. When tragedy comes, the Care Pastors are the ones they seek. And since people are different, and needs vary, it is not possible to mention all instances. Allow the Holy Spirit to lead you and build relationships with your flock to the point where opportunities become apparent to you. Simply following the *Five Points of Contact*, to which you will be introduced later, will create many ways and means for providing meaningful ministry.

So, whether you are a pastor, a leader, an active member or a senior, healthy or sick, everyone needs to receive care. And no one should not have to first face a crisis to receive love and care either.

Jesus, Our Model

The ministry of Jesus was known by miracles, signs, and wonders and included a great deal of teaching, training, and praying. Yet the Bible says Jesus was grieved and moved by compassion. Why? Because He saw the people "as sheep without a shepherd"— people who were not cared for (Matthew 9:35-37). After Jesus had done all the *spiritual work*, there was still a vacuum. There was a need for the ministry of *compassion*. The modern-day church by and large has missed this powerful principle of *intentional care*, which should follow our teaching and preaching.

Developing people spiritually and caring for them lovingly should never oppose each other. They should function hand-in-hand and side-by-side. The church must look outward as they look inward. If you neglect the "in-reach" you will never have an "outreach."

3

DEVELOPING THE CARE MINISTRY NETWORK

Introduction

In this chapter, we are going to focus our attention on preparing for the launch and describe how the *Care Ministry Network* fits jointly together. We want to assure that God's people are well-equipped to care for one another.

We refer to the *concept* of our care ministry as *Congregational Care*, and generally refer to those who provide the ministry as, Care *Shepherds* and Care *Pastors*. The entire ministry is referred to as **The Care Ministry Network.** In a local church, it is often simply referred to as *Care Ministry* and identified by the church's name, e.g., *Life Church Care Ministry.*

We will get to it again later, but I don't want you to get bogged down with names, titles, and descriptions at this point. If you don't like what we call our care partners, then hold on, we will help you with suggested alternatives.[12] Just do not ditch the whole idea of congregational care simply because you are not comfortable with calling your workers *care pastors* or *care shepherds*. It's the *concept* that's important, not the labels. Care ministry is about a *towel*, not a *title*.

> Care ministry
> is *about a towel,*
> *not a title.*

Developing the Care Ministry Structure

Conceptual Stage

During the conceptual stage of launching the *Care Ministry Network,* it is vital that the Lead Pastor still be involved in most of the discussions. If the pastor seems detached from developing the care system, it will most assuredly not get off the ground. Although it should be run by the church members eventually, it must be initiated by the pastor originally.

The early considerations of launching a care ministry normally starts with staff and board members but should also include a select group of people out of the membership early on. Select approximately five (depending on the size of the church) enthusiastic church members who have a clear interest in caring for people and possess some organizational skills.

---

12   See page 91

Although every church will structure its care ministry based on their personal needs, the following may serve as a helpful outline to formulate the ministry functions:

1. The starting point for all should be to read the book, *Care Revolution*. Inspire those who are going to be part of your launch group (and even your church and staff leadership team) to each read through the book twice to have a good understanding of the hypothesis of congregational care provided by members.
2. At the first meeting, ask each person present to briefly relate their understanding of congregational care as presented in the *Care Revolution*.
3. The next step is to have the Lead Pastor discuss his/her vision for the ministry and especially highlight the positive things that will come out of this concept.
4. Have a moment of questions and answers. (This is why we have provided abundant information for pastors in the *Care Revolution* book).
5. Begin to formulate your mission and vision for your care ministry.
6. Have a calendar handy and begin to design your plans for implementation, although some events may still be flexible. In general, pinpoint the date when the vision will be shared with the congregation, inform how further marketing will be developed, and share when the training conference will be presented (where, by whom, schedules, acquisition of material, and more).

Be very careful though, to not kill the vision by spending unnecessary amounts of time in the finer details. Sometimes we get so bogged down in the specifics, wanting to make sure we cross every "t", and dot every "i", that we lose sight of the ultimate goal. Be focused, be prepared, and be ready.

Later on in this chapter, we will introduce the need for an ongoing *leadership team*. The people involved in the above discussions, or at least some of them, would be ideal candidates to place in this role. It will be most helpful in providing continuity.

Casting the Vision

The first action step of the initial launch, after you have spent adequate time in the above discussions, is to share the vision with the congregation. It works best when spread over three to four weekends. The first should be an introduction to the care ministry concept, sharing as many positive highlights as possible. This should be followed by a series of three messages over three weekends, based on the importance of congregational care, involving church members in actual works of ministry, the joys of caring, and more.

Drawing the Net

Immediately after the third message (on the same day), while the iron is hot, people should be given the opportunity to sign up to attend the *Care Pastors Training Conference*. Invite as many people as possible to attend the conference, regardless of whether they know they are going to be involved in the ministry or not. The more people are exposed to the actual workings of the ministry, the easier it will be to implement the ministry.

The Training Conference

The *Care Pastors Training Conference* becomes one of the pinnacles of the entire preparation process. Promote it thoroughly, plan it well, and set the stage for great success. You simply cannot afford to not have a well-organized conference. This is where you set the standard of expectation for your care ministry.

Since the Care Ministry Network is largely a new concept to most churches, we recommend that pastors and churches, for their initial launch, consult with CMNi. They can provide trainers to help you equip your people or simply provide advice or answer questions. CMNi serves as a network, providing assistance to those churches that develop their own Care Ministry Network. Think of CMNi as the Care Pastors to churches around the world. By connecting with CMNi Central, a channel of communication is created for easier dialogue between them and you, especially over the crucial first year.

Launch

After the conclusion of the training conference, those who have been chosen and have declared their willingness to serve as Care Pastors should be commissioned on a Sunday morning in the presence of the entire congregation. This then becomes the big event — the great announcement of the official launch of the *Care Ministry Network* in the congregation. After this, the Care Pastors are released to do the work of the ministry as they were authorized and instructed.

Let all things be done decently and in order.
1 Corinthians 14:40.

Designing the Structure

DEFINITION: The Care Ministry Network is an authentic and proven congregational care system that enables God's people to care for one another.

There is probably not much more that can be added to this description of the care ministry. It is plain, simple, and to the point. It will be most helpful for everyone to memorize the definition and be able to easily recite it. The reason for this is that more and more people in the church are going to hear about the care ministry and will normally begin to ask what the concept means. Instead of fumbling, or looking for an explanation, the easiest answer will be to repeat the definition. But ... be careful to not recite it like a first grader!

PLEASE NOTE the essence of the Care Ministry Network:

1. *... An authentic system ...* This means it is not an added-on program, but rather a classification that becomes part of a congregation's DNA. It cultivates a culture of care to the point where a church could potentially become known as *The Caring Place*. It implies a realistic and meaningful purpose that has substance in its implementation.

2. *... Congregational care ...* The importance of this aspect is that it underscores the fact that this ministry is not meant for an exclusive few, but rather for all who are part of the congregation. *Caring* becomes the glue that connects people to each other. Programs may *attract* people, but do not *connect* people. Caring provides the *Velcro* every church needs. Once people connect, it's hard for them to leave.

3. ... *Which enables God's people* ... This is a ministry for the believers to the believers. It is does not run on the feet of the vocational ministers (clergy), but on the feet of the people (Laos) — the church members. At its core the care ministry aims to identify, develop, and release believers to function in meaningful roles of ministry.
4. ... *To Care for one another* ... This concept is a powerful and Biblical way of making sure that all members are connected to each other and that no one falls through the cracks. People are cared for in the good times as well as the bad. It is not necessarily an evangelism ministry, but certainly has some elements thereof in its application. Church health and Church growth is a natural outflow of a care ministry.

Our system does not only provide a relational element, it also creates ways for people to systematically become involved in the life of the church. *The Care Ministry Network* solidifies a church, brings unity, and ensures cohesiveness. It's not so much about in-reach as it is about outreach. I have stated previously that every living body functions on eleven different systems and if one of these systems break down, the body becomes ill and loses its strength and energy. The ministry of care is one such system in the body of Christ, and when it breaks down, the congregation becomes ill and loses its strength and energy to reach out in evangelism, missions, outreaches, and other ministry activities. That is why I emphasize that our focus is not on building our churches larger, but instead, making them healthier.

4

PUTTING THE NETWORK TOGETHER

THE FIVE BASIC LEVELS OF THE CARE MINISTRY NETWORK

The *Care Ministry Network* encompasses five basic levels of leadership. These levels are important to effectively execute and sustain the ministry.

The five levels we are referring to are as follows:
1. Care Director
2. Care Leadership Team
3. Care Shepherds
4. Care Pastors
5. Flocks (Family Groups)

By now it should be clear that our Care Ministry is a *member-driven* ministry. That, of course, does not mean that they are cut loose to function independently and do whatever they desire. They should clearly be operating under the authority of the Lead Pastor and be accountable to him or her according to the prescribed system.

Let's be clear: This is not a haphazard, loosely organized ministry. While it is not our intention to develop such a rigid organization wherein nobody has freedom to function, we do advocate the importance of operating in accordance to a well-designed structure that has levels of answerability. As Paul says in Ephesians 4:16, "The whole body fitly joined together and compacted by that which every joint supplies . . ."

THESE ARE THE PEOPLE YOU ARE GOING TO NEED

1. The Care Director

After the goals of the ministry have been determined by a *launch group* as mentioned above, the first person that should be identified and appointed is the Care Ministry Director. It is advisable, however *not mandatory*, to have had this person be part of the initial discussions and would know the expectations of the leadership.

After having observed many churches across the nation, it has become abundantly clear that much of the ongoing success and effectiveness of the care ministry depends heavily upon the person who will be directing its affairs. Someone must lead the ministry and it should not be the pastor. Find a couple to lead your care ministry who is contagiously enthusiastic about caring for other people. They will play a major role in recruiting your leadership team and promoting the concept to the wider body.

The director *could* be a vocational minister, but that does not have to be the case. In most churches, it remains a volunteer position, but in larger churches it usually requires persons who can devote most of their time to the ministry. The Care Director should primarily have a heart for people and clearly exhibit organizational and leadership skills.

Take time to find the correct person(s) (preferably a couple) and spend personal, quality time to train and equip them on leadership principles and organizational skills. The more time spent at the outset, the more the chance of success will be assured in the long run. Initially, it will ask for time investment but the benefits from it will be well worth the effort. The closer the tie between the Lead Pastor and the Care Ministry Director, the more effective the ministry will be.

The Care Ministry Director leads the Care Leadership Team (described below), is responsible for leading the Care Ministry Network, and is directly accountable to the Lead Pastor. Relying again on meaningful feedback, it is vitally important that the pastor remains the director's greatest cheer leader and encourager. The greatest gift a pastor can give the Care Director (and the ministry as a whole) is to keep the ministry *alive* from the pulpit and encourage people to become involved.

Since leading the care ministry will take much time and energy, it is strongly recommended that the director, whether full-time or part-time, be devoted exclusively to the Care Ministry Network and not be involved in any other ministry leadership position.

In cases where churches have fifty or less members, pastors have for the most part chosen to take on the role of the Care Director until the ministry has grown sufficiently.

2. The Care Leadership Team

Select three to five, at most seven (depending on the size of your church), lay people in the congregation who exhibit the gift of mercy and noticeably have compassion for people. It will be most helpful if they have some leadership and organizational skills. As mentioned previously, it may be the best part of wisdom to select some of the people who were part of the initial discussion group to function in this capacity. In summary, their task will primarily revolve around working with the director to help design strategy for the successful implementation and ongoing operation of the care ministry.

The Care Leadership Team, as is the case with the director, should preferably also be selected and appointed before the actual launch of the ministry. If this team cannot be appointed before the *Care Pastors Training Conference,* it is not a crisis. Many times, these individuals are best identified by their enthusiasm and attitudes during the conference itself and then appointed immediately before the actual launch of the ministry. But the pastor should be sure to pray and ask the Holy Spirit for guidance and discernment as to whom should be appointed in these roles.

A point of clarity: While recruiting, preparing, and coaching the leadership team, the Lead Pastor should preferably still be closely involved. This is important, because it is in this phase, the laying of the foundation, that the heart and vision of the pastor is knit into the ongoing fabric of the entire care ministry. After the ministry has taken off, the pastor discreetly withdraws from immediate involvement and delegates the responsibility to the director and team.

The Leadership Team should clearly understand the expectation of the pastor. Of course, most of the theology and philosophy is described in the *Care Revolution* and will greatly shape the thinking of the pastor and team alike on the subject. It goes without saying that each of the members of the leadership team should have their own copy of the *Care Revolution,* and thoroughly familiarize themselves with its content. It should form part of their training and preparation.

Take time to solidify the leadership team and have them unify around the corporate goal of what needs to be accomplished. It is vitally important that this group completely understands what the care ministry is all about and can answer any questions that are directed to them. Their unified voice will be very helpful when officially launching this ministry. Here also, it is highly recommended that the leadership team members not be overly involved in other ministry responsibilities.

The Care Leadership Team functions under the delegated authority of the Official Board of the church and has jurisdiction only as far as it pertains to the *Care Ministry Network*. The Leadership Team should appoint a person from among them to serve as secretary.

Although the leadership team, under the direction of the care director, will lead the entire ministry, it can never be separated from the Lead Pastor. They can ignore the leadership of their pastor as little as the musicians of a symphony orchestra can ignore the directions of its conductor.

When One Actually Means Two

When it comes to the Leadership Team, we have *individuals* in mind to serve in this role. When it comes to the other positions, however, we usually refer to it in the singular but uphold the plural. I know that does not make sense, so let me explain:

When we reference people such as the director, or a care shepherd, or a care pastor, we are in fact suggesting a couple — a husband/wife team, or two single people joining together for the ministry. We never want people to function independently or individually in this ministry. So, even if we do talk about a *care pastor* (singular), we have two people in mind.

3. Care Shepherds

Care Shepherds function in a supervisory or mentorship capacity. They are directly accountable to the Care Ministry Director and are each assigned five Care Pastors for whom they are responsible. They function in a peer relationship with the other Care Shepherds.

Other than operating in these leadership and advisory roles, the Care Shepherds primarily function as the care pastors to the Care Pastors and apply the same *Points of Contact* (which will be explained in detail later) to them. Their role is primarily twofold:

(1) To provide ministry *mentorship*, and
(2) To serve as a *shepherd* (to the Care Pastors).

There are few things that are so encouraging and motivating to a Care Pastor as the healthy relationship with a caring and understanding Care Shepherd. The role of a Care Shepherd is invaluable in the entire process of making a church healthy.

Dr. Kenneth Pohly nailed it when he gave the following definition of a Care Shepherd (Mentor):

> "Pastoral supervision [mentoring] is a method of doing and reflecting on ministry in which a shepherd and one or more lay pastors [Care Pastors] covenant together to reflect critically on their ministry as a way of growing in self-

awareness, competence, biblical understanding and Christian Commitment."[13]

Selecting Care Shepherds

The Care Director and Leadership Team are responsible for identifying potential Care Shepherds and recommend them to the Lead Pastor. Potential Care Shepherds are required to undergo specialized training by means of attending a conference called the *Advanced Leadership Conference.*

Smaller churches may choose to initially not engage the level of Care Shepherds but instead have the Director or even one or two of the Leadership Team Members fulfill this role where needed.

Progression

Best practice is for the Care Shepherds to initially serve as Care Pastors before they are appointed to serve as Care Shepherds. (The first-time launch may be different). It just makes good sense to have them experience first-hand what it's like to be a Care Pastor. It could potentially be very difficult for them to mentor their respective Care Pastors if they themselves have never faced the challenges that generally come naturally when serving other people. Nothing is as educational as personal experience. When Care Pastors do advance to become Care Shepherds, there obviously should be qualified people who can step up to take over the role of the outgoing Care Pastor.

Some churches find they have an ample supply of good and capable leaders who could adapt to the role of a Care Shepherd quite

---

13 Pohly, Kenneth H. *Pastoral Supervision.* Houston: The Institute of Religion, 1977.

easily. They felt comfortable putting them through the *Advanced Leadership Conference* shortly after they had attended the *Care Pastors Training Conference*. I have not heard of any serious complaints. We do not run by the law of the Medes and the Persians; whatever fits your church and your people will be just fine.

> Poor preparation
> results in
> poor performance

Since the role and ministry of a Care Shepherd is rather specialized, we will not deal with all the aspects of leadership, qualifications, functions, duties, and applications in this book.[14]

4. Care Pastors

Care Pastors can truly be called the champions of the care ministry. They are indispensable to the success of the concept. They are the ones who essentially connect with their fellow church members, build relationships, and provide the ongoing care. Everything we do in the *Care Ministry Network* flows through them. That is the reason why they need to be thoroughly prepared for the task.

Care Pastors are accountable and relate to the Care Shepherds and each have a *Flock* (described below) for whom they are responsible. They are in a peer relationship with the other Care Pastors. They are purposefully trained and equipped to function as care pastors to

---

14   Complete and separate training guides are utilized to prepare, equip, and develop Care Shepherds to function in their unique ministry at the *Advanced Leadership Conference*. It fully describes all the prerequisites for a Care Shepherd and serves to thoroughly mature them for their ministry.

provide effective care to the group of people to whom they have been assigned.

You Should Have Both

The information we provide in the *Handbook* lays the groundwork for the *Care Pastors Training Conference* and simultaneously introduces important models for care pastors to follow. Although this handbook provides detailed information not to be found anywhere else, we also know it is not practical to attempt to equip people out of a book such as this alone — therefore, we have designed a specific training guide, known as the *Care Pastor Participant's Guide* which can be found on our website.

> You should have both:
> this textbook and
> the training guides.

The *Participant's Guide* often cites page numbers as references back to the handbook. (E.g. H.B. 37 will mean page 37 in this handbook). This is done to undergird the teaching with more in-depth information to provide complete content. To sufficiently train and prepare care pastors, each participant should have both the *Handbook* and the training guide.

Assistant Care Pastors

One of the first very exciting things care pastors experience, after their commissioning, is getting to know the people who have been assigned to them. This is truly an adventure and a joyful experience. Many care pastors have discovered in this process a newfound appreciation for their own pastor. They soon realize that not even *they* can do it alone. Ministry always looks different from the outside in than it does from the inside out.

Soon after Care Pastors have met their respective families, they should identify *Assistant Care Pastors*. They should look to recognize a suitable "couple" who has the abilities and the desire to be involved in caring for others. They should initially begin by working alongside their care pastor couple and then attend a *Training Conference* at the next available opportunity.

The thought behind this is that these Assistant Care Pastors will eventually be assigned their own flock after being commissioned. A good example of this is when a *Flock* (group of families) grow to become, say eight family units, they multiply into two groups — the assistant care pastor (now commissioned as a care pastor) takes five families and the original care pastor takes three (since they have more experience and could build out the flock again.) This form of succession helps alleviate the disappointment when families have become endeared to their Care Pastor and a new group is formed.

Having an assistant couple also helps fill the vacuum in cases where the Care Pastor is appointed as a Care Shepherd. The Assistant Care Pastor in this way is not a stranger to the flock and relationships have already been built. These trained assistants can therefore readily take over from their leader.

When new members are added to the church and sufficient Care Pastors are not available, Assistant Care Pastors who have been equipped (and who have not yet been assigned), then become the leaders of a newly formed flock. This multiplication helps to keep the care ministry dynamic and vibrant. These changes should be done at the recommendation of the Care Shepherd and the approval of the Care Director.

Tenure of Care Pastors

Care Pastors are initially asked to serve a one-year term. Although much cannot normally be accomplished in such a short span of time, it does provide an *out* on both sides. It allows the couple to determine if they are a fit for the ministry, while, on the other hand, allows the leadership to recommend an alternative ministry to couples who are seemingly not being effective. In most cases, we have found that care pastors choose to stay involved for an extended period of time. They enjoy the ministry and find much fulfillment in their responsibilities.

The One-year Cycle

The first year of implementing the care ministry is typically the most exciting — and the most challenging at the same time. It's a new concept and has to of necessity be adopted into the DNA of the church. This often takes time. The ministry takes off with great anticipation and then after six or seven months, while most are still running forward with enthusiasm, for others reality seems to set in. Some admit it's not as glamorous as they thought and that it really means getting out of their comfort zones.

So, if you find attrition of Care Pastors during the first year, do not be alarmed. You're not doing anything wrong. Be patient, because you will find the people who truly have a heart for the ministry always remain. It is usually also at this point that others, who have thus far not been part of the ministry, step forward, because they have seen the great results of the concept and want to be part of the progression.

After the ministry has been in existence for a full ministry year, it is usually a good time to consider some changes. These changes must be made with careful thought and sincere prayer. Unless it is absolutely necessary, care pastors should not be assigned to a *new* flock, neither should family groups be placed under a different care pastor just for the sake of rotation. People become attached to their care pastor and care pastors become close to their people. And this is good, because the whole purpose of the care concept is to build community and develop relationships. It takes time to establish these kinds of bonds and would cause more hurt than help to force unnecessary adjustments. Once trust is built, you don't want to cast that into the wind. Relationships are built on trust. Leave people in place as much as possible and as far as it is healthy for the furtherance of the overall ministry.

Sometimes, however, it becomes necessary to make some modification, and that is quite in order. Families who simply do not connect with their care pastor will reap no benefit from the ministry relationship. It will be best to place them under the care of another couple.

Then, in rare cases, a Care Pastor may not be able to relate to a family or individual. After having tried for twelve months it may be wise to make adjustments. Do not however, make any changes from the *top* (leadership team) without consulting with the care pastors on the ground level first. The same applies when the leadership desires to move families from one flock to another. It should be done with discretion and by discussing it with the involved families and care pastors alike. Never make a *cold decision* in a leadership meeting and simply pass the instructions down. We are working hard in connecting people and certainly do not want to disrupt the relationships.

Strange as it may seem, on the other hand, we have received feedback from some Care Pastors who said they did not want the *difficult* family taken from them. "Perhaps I need to learn something from this relationship," one said. "I have wondered if the problem is me, rather than the family." In another case, consulting with their Care

Shepherd, a couple sincerely said, "please give us some more time. This may be a character lesson we have to learn." Their requests were honored, and today they are the greatest of friends. So, don't be too regimented in your thinking. Listen, observe, and be sure to follow the leadership of the Holy Spirit. This ministry is dynamic, vibrant, and organic and if allowed, will take on an identity of its own in every congregation.

It may sound contradictory to everything I just said, but I need to add that in some rare cases churches wanted their family groups to change from Care Pastors after every twelve-month cycle. Their reasons differ, and in many cases have merit. I mention this simply because I want to make all options available and to not let it sound as though we are operating under a rigid ruling. Let culture, convenience, and circumstance determine what's best. I do want to underscore the caution that it is not recommended to make changes just for changes sake.

5. A Flock

This obviously is the level where the actual ministry takes place and where our energy is mostly spent. A Flock, or family group, normally consists of three to five family units under the watchfulness of a Care Pastor. (In some cases, more than five families have to be assigned to a Care Pastor — but take care that they do not become overwhelmed).

A family unit may consist of a father/mother with children, a couple, or even a single person living on his or her own. We want to underscore the necessity of not only providing care to families but also to single persons.

People are eligible to be taken up in a flock the moment they become members of the congregation. The *Care Ministry Network* is designed specifically to serve the membership — the household of faith.

After people have crossed the bridge from *connection* to *commitment (covenant)*, they become part of the church community where we provide authentic pastoral care to each one and make sure that none of our people are neglected. They never simply become names in a database, but rather valuable members who are part of the body of Christ.[15]

New Members: Connect Them

Engaging new members with a Care Pastor is the first step in ensuring stability, creating a sense of belonging, and confirming acceptance. This process is more important than most people may realize at the outset. It has become obvious, in so many churches, that after people have become members, they are typically left to themselves to find their own way through the maze of ministries to hopefully connect with fellow members. That is the greatest reason for such a high percentage of member attrition in our churches. If you don't have a way of embracing your new members and connecting them with the process of your church's development, they will not stay.

If taken into consideration how we doted on them when they first came, and the attention we gave them by means of free gifts, or coffee at the café, letters we have sent them, and the red carpet we rolled out at the new member's conference, it is easy to see how they can feel let down when suddenly nobody pays any attention to them and they then assume they are indeed mere names in a database.

---

15 Refer to the *Care Revolution,* page 249 for insightful discussion on church membership.

> It's different when
> People are connected to
> The Care Ministry

Here's the Difference

A church that has the *Care Ministry Network* in place explains the care concept during their new member's orientation event and connects new families to an already trained Care Pastor couple who embraces them and guides them in their growth process.

Our purpose is never to just add members to our congregation, but to help them become acquainted with the church family, connect with our discipleship process, and find a place of ministry that fits their giftedness. Once this happens, new members become bonded to the church and its mission. The result is a healthy church — and a healthy church has much more ability to positively impact its community and the world.

Then There Are Others

Some people attend our churches but clearly do not want to commit to membership; at least not at the outset. They want to remain in the shadows. Other times, the reason for their coming to our church is to hide in the corners of the unfamiliar. We need to respect that. For these reasons, and many more, we don't embarrass people by forcing *care* upon them. We allow them to set the parameters and choose their level of engagement. But when people covenant to membership, they also assign responsibility to us to make sure we care about them.

Then there are people that have been part of the congregation for the longest time but have, for some reason or another, never become members and probably never will. They are faithful in attendance; financially support the church and are even involved in ministry. It will obviously be a grave mistake to exclude them from receiving care. Include them into your flocks and assign them to a Care Pastor. One of the *last things* you want to do is hurt or estrange people. If you are going to err, do so on the side of being gracious rather than on the side of being rigorous.

CARE MINISTRY STRUCTURE

The following graphic will help you better understand the levels of leadership and how the entire structure is knit together:

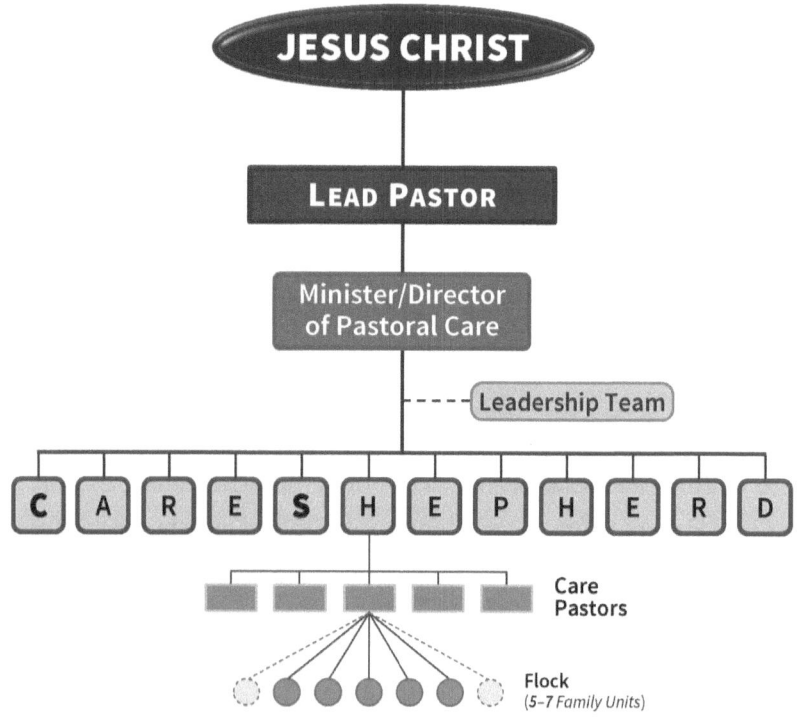

Organizational chart for the Care Pastors network

The functions and strategies for Care Pastors and Care Shepherds will be more fully described in Chapter 6, entitled *The Contact System*.

Alternative Descriptions

Since I am aware that some pastors and churches may not be comfortable to use the title descriptions I have chosen, it may be helpful to suggest some alternatives to consider:

1. Care Ministry Network
   - Care Ministry
   - Connect Ministry
   - Community Groups
   - Care Group Ministry
   - iCare Ministry

2. Care Ministry Director
   - Care Director
   - Community Care Leader
   - Care Group Leader
   - iCare Director

3. Care Shepherds
   - Care Supervisors
   - Care Leaders
   - iCare Supervisors

4. Care Pastors
   - Care Group Leaders
   - Community Care Leaders
   - Connect Leaders
   - Care Ministers
   - iCare Ministers

5. Flocks   Family Groups
             Care Groups
             Clusters
             iCare Groups

5

THE ROLE OF THE CARE PASTOR

The C.A.R.E Module

The heart of the *Care Ministry Network* can best be described by the acronym *C-A-R-E*. These four areas described by this ellipsis are what a Care Pastor does and also tell us what this ministry is all about. *C-A-R-E* describes the functions required by each member of the entire care team — not just the Care Pastors. I am devoting an entire chapter to this segment because all of what we envision to encompass in our care ministry flows from these four qualities. *C-A-R-E* can aptly also be described as the job description of the Care Pastors.

If these four commitments are performed effectively, quality care will be the result in every church. If we take "care" out of the equation, labor is all that is left. We want the C.A.R.E culture to become so evident that our church will become known as *The Caring Place!* The "Contact System" we describe in Chapter Six is the elaboration of these four expectations.

The Application of C-A-R-E

Let's start off by clarifying each of these segments with a one-line description. It always makes it easier to comprehend, and more importantly, to remember.

C—Contact each family on a regular basis
A—Availability - be available to your flock
R—Reach out in prayer on behalf of each family consistently
E—Exemplify a Christian lifestyle - be an example

Contact

The fundamental expectation is for Care Pastors to make a minimum of one *personal contact* per month with each family who is under their care. They can do this by means of a personal visit to people's home, if acceptable, or at minimum, a meaningful phone call with purpose. Your role is to be pastoral, which means displaying care and concern, creating acceptance, and showing love.

When Care Pastors make their *first contact* with their families, however, the meeting should be a one-on-one, eye-to-eye visit. You should not make this particular contact by means of a phone call, email, text, or whatever other way. The main purpose of the first contact is to get acquainted, explain the ministry and clarify expectations of the relationship. Thereafter the "Five Points of Contact" should be followed.

It's incredibly difficult to build a relationship with anyone without having first made a personal contact. You can never develop a relationship from a distance. You can only do so up close. Your entire ministry effort becomes very easy once you meet the people you are going to serve, not only now, but also in the future. We start our ministry involvement with contact and then continue with contact.

Note: In this *module discussion* we are only dealing with the *fact* that we have to develop contacts, but later in Chapter Six, we will describe *how* contacts should be made and how contact should be maintained.

Availability

If building relationships is what community is all about, then availability seems to be the obvious requirement for Care Pastors. Being *available* also means being *accessible*. You should be available to your flock members when they have personal concerns they would like to share with you, or when they simply want to talk. Be very visible especially on Sundays and other times of church gatherings — before, during, and after each service. This means that you should come to church early, and stay late, rather than come late and leave early.

Being available also requires Care Pastors to provide their flock members with their contact information, including telephone numbers, email address, etc. Integrity will demand that Care Pastors receive and/or return calls. I have, at times, heard the reluctance of Care Pastors to provide their phone numbers to their flocks. Remember, you are not handing out your information to everybody and his brother. You are giving it to your trusted friends. So, share your contact information and stay available.

Many churches provide their Care Pastors with pre-printed cards that have the church's name, address, and contact information on it, plus the name and contact information of the Care Pastor. This is not only helpful to hand to flock members, but a helpful tool for hospital visitation and other occasions.

Care Pastors should be willing to assist their people in any way possible. If you cannot provide the help they need, make every attempt to connect them with someone who can and be sure to follow through. Or, find the answer and pass it along to the inquirer. Being a helpful channel in this way only helps to strengthen relationships.

Reach out in prayer

Prayer should be the priority of a Care Pastor's ministry. As Mel Steinbron says, "If prayer is all the pastoring some people receive, it's already more than most are getting." At times you may find people who would say, "Don't visit me," but you will never find anyone who would say, "Don't pray for me."

Praying for your group each by name has great results:
- *It develops a joint concern* for the burdens and needs for your flock members. You begin to feel their passion.
- *It silently establishes a bond.* You simply cannot help to sense closeness to a person you are praying for in sincerity on a regular basis.
- *It deepens a sense of accountability.* Through your efforts of praying for your people in sincere devotion, it allows God the opportunity to lay the burden of care and concern squarely upon your shoulders and infuses you with divine love for them.
- *It is a productive time between God and you.* Not only do these moments of prayer avail Care Pastors the opportunity to pray for their flock members, but the warmth of the atmosphere also creates precious moments that God could speak to them intimately.

- *It becomes the catalyst that keeps you able to function.* Prayer is the key to be an effective Care Pastor. There is no way that any person could lose passion for the care ministry if they have developed disciplined prayer for their flock members. When you stop praying, you will stop pastoring. I have often found that people who become discouraged in their ministry efforts are those who are not committed in prayer for their people.

Pray for your
People
Every day!

Care Pastors are encouraged to pray for their people every day. This could very well be one of the most important things they can do for them. When we pray for people with love, devotion, and compassion the Holy Spirit will help us understand what they are facing and guide us in the best way we can minister to them.

As Christians, we know we are also people of the Spirit. If we remain very sensitive to the whisper of the Holy Spirit, while praying for an individual or couple, He will lead and guide us to understand exactly how to pray and even what to pray for. In that way, we will be able to minister to our people on a much higher level. An encouraging call from you at the right moment may make a world of difference to a discouraged member.

A great way to be effective in your prayers for your families is to instead of praying for them generally, to instead pray for only one family per day and zero in on them. Mention them by name, one-by-one, and allow the Holy Spirit to direct you.

Exemplify a Christian Lifestyle

It almost sounds superfluous to say, but Care Pastors should be an example to their people all the time. Not only at church events, or within their flock, but every day of the week, wherever they go. People may see or hear you at times and places you don't even realize. Watch what you say and do at the grocery store, at the cashier's desk, in the parking lot, at a traffic light, etc. Care Pastors should also guard what they say about other people — including criticism of their pastor, church leaders or other church members.

> 1 Timothy 4:12 says, ". . . be an example to the believers, in word, in conversation, in charity, in spirit, in faith, in purity."

> 1 Thessalonians 5:22 admonish us to "Abstain from all appearance of evil."

Reality Fact: You can fail on the first three areas of C-A-R-E and may possibly even get away with it — at least for a while — but if you fail in being an example, you will assuredly lose the confidence or support of your people. They simply won't trust you and the fruit of your ministry will be minimal. I realize the great responsibility it places on a Care Pastor, but then, we should all as Christians already live exemplary lives in any case.

Being an example should not imply that the Care Pastor is perfect, superior to the flock member, more mature, or even more qualified. It does suggest the need to be humble, faithful, and unselfish. It also suggests that we are all friends traveling the same road to the same destiny, learning from one another how to grow and develop spiritually. Friendship, relationship, and companionship — they all lead to mutual ministry. Through camaraderie people give something of themselves to each other. We can all learn from one another.

C-A-R-E for Your Flock Members All the Time

Build relationships with your flock without overwhelming them. Be available, but never intrude in their personal lives without invitation. Being accessible and approachable on a constant basis will build confidence and strengthen the bonds of connection. Be careful to not let your people feel they are being "watched" all the time. Instead, give them the sense they are important enough to receive attention.

Although not quoted verbatim, Mel Steinbron says, it is just as important to care for people when there are no critical problems in their lives as when there are, for it is the relationship that is built in non-crisis times that earns Care Pastors the right to be trusted during the hurting times.

A Simple Process to Follow

After the Lead Pastor has cast the vision for launching a Care Ministry Network in the congregation, the following brief steps are suggested:

- Those members interested are invited to an orientation meeting, led by the Care Ministry Director, with the Lead Pastor as the catalyst speaker.
- Prospective candidates will be encouraged to take a *Spiritual Gifts Inventory Test* — if they have not recently already done so.
- Each potential Care Pastor should purchase and read the textbook, the *Care Revolution,* and make an in-depth

study of the contents. Reading this material will save enormous time when the pastor gets ready to describes the concept.
- They will be required to enroll to attend and complete a *Care Pastors Training Conference.*
- If selected, they will have the opportunity to declare their willingness to serve as a care pastor for at least twelve months.
- Care Pastors will be publicly commissioned by the laying on of hands by the elders of the church. (Details will be explained as we proceed.)
- They will be assigned a flock of five to seven family units of which they may potentially request three.
- They should diligently follow through with their ministry commitment.
- They should follow the leadership and instructions of their mentors and coaches.
- Care Pastors should attend all *Care Ministry Network* events.

DEVELOPING A COMMON UNDERSTANDING

As pastors, we do not take the role of the Care Pastor lightly. We fully realize that we are entrusting the lives of precious people to them and have to build careful expectations into the relationship we develop with our Care Pastors. They are representing Christ, His Church, their Pastor, and the congregation-at-large. It is important that Care Pastors continue to function under the delegated authority of their church leaders and be willing to take on the responsibility of caring for the families assigned to them.

Desiring to become the best Care Pastors they can be, they will pursue great relations with their fellow workers and strive to continually be trained and developed in their ministry. Congregational care is so vibrant and life-giving that everything we do in this regard enhances the spiritual climate in our churches. It is in this kind of atmosphere that a church becomes healthy which results in it becoming conducive to evangelism and missions.

Since we place such a huge appreciation on the ministry of Care Pastors, the following points are to be considered as a common understanding to function effectively:

- Be willing to function according to the C-A-R-E Module.
- Surrender yourself sincerely to the Lordship of Jesus Christ and the authority of your church.
- Be willing to make time and energy available to perform your ministry.
- Make yourself willing and available to serve in your role for as long as the Lord leads.
- Be willing to receive ongoing training and development.
- Be willing to submit to accountability.
- Conduct yourself at all times in a manner consistent with biblical principles of holiness, and in a manner that will serve as an example for others to follow.
- Develop an ongoing lifestyle of ministry and servitude, allowing every occasion to be available to God for touching the lives of others in every area of your life.

Standard of Commitment

These commitments determine the effectiveness of the ministry and should be held high in high expectation. If these understandings are lowered, the importance and helpfulness of the care ministry will decrease, the quality will decline, and so will the morale of the people. The Care Director and Leadership Team should always work hard on keeping these standards high by creating an atmosphere of excitement and self-realization. Always make time to show appreciation and affirm Care Pastors when they are doing well.

The way accountability is built into the process is by means of monthly reports the Care Pastors have to turn in to their Care Shepherds. The latter should turn in their reports to the Care Director. If there is no accountability, the entire ministry is doomed to failure. It is the only way whereby the leaders can evaluate the functions of the ministry and design further development. The bottom-line expectation is communication, which is the only instrument for gauging progress and/or determining adjustments.

Character Commitment

In ministry we tend to view the goal as the goal, but in God's economy, the *process* is the goal. It's not about what we're doing at all; it's about who we're becoming in the process. (Mark Batterson)

Character development is an ongoing progression and is oftentimes honed and shaped as we face the challenges of life. What we ARE is more important than what we DO.

BEING precedes DOING!

Care Pastors need to be developed at two stages:
- Firstly, who they ARE, and
- Secondly, what they DO.

It is easier to learn what to *do* than it is to allow the Holy Spirit to shape us in what we should *be*.

We who are in ministry need to work on what we do, but we need to work harder on what we are. I find more and more in my personal life that I am asking God to make me a loving person rather than helping me to love people, to make me a patient person rather than enabling me to show patience, to make me a compassionate person rather than to have compassion, to make me a servant rather than helping me to serve people, to make me a generous person rather than helping me give more.[16]

> We should be committed to
> *BECOMING* the people of God
> Before *DOING* the work of God

Loving and caring have to be a way of life, not functions of a program we may do at times.

Matthew 7:17-18 says, "Every sound tree bears good fruit . . . a sound tree cannot bear evil fruit." A healthy tree will always produce good fruit.

Choosing to be a *servant* is more important than choosing to be *served*.

---

16 Melvin J. Steinbron, *Can the Pastor do it Alone.* Wipf and Stock, Eugene, OR, 2004. P98.

"Just as the Son of Man did not come to be served, but to serve . . ." Matthew 20:28 (NKJV).

In 1Timothy Chapter 3 (where ministry qualifications are discussed), *"BE"* is written eight times and implied fifteen times. People understand the teaching they can *see* in the life of the one who is teaching. People will do best that which they can see exemplified in the life of the one who is with them.

Personal godliness is the most powerful ministry tool. But it takes time and energy to develop.

6

THE CONTACT SYSTEM

In this chapter, we are going to focus our attention on explaining the nuts and bolts of the actual implementation of the Care Pastor's assignment. Everything that has been discussed thus far was all in preparation to come to this point. These points of contact are the crux of the ministry of pastoral care in the local church and are the elaborations of the *C-A-R-E Module* described in Chapter Five.

Contact is the only way to establish a relationship with someone else and thus becomes the "glue" that holds the entire ministry together. It becomes the bonding agent that causes people become united. In a time when calendars have become hectic and schedules have become overloaded, more and more people have become reclusive. The digital age, as useful as it is, has not helped to solve this problem.

The Care Pastor's ministry is one of presence. It can never be performed from a distance. We are earnestly seeking to build community by developing meaningful relationships. Because the true character of a shepherd is required to be an effective Care Pastor, we need to seek for people who have a heart that protects, cares, nurtures, encourages, and guides.

When a culture of care prevails in a congregation and people know they are accepted and sense that they belong, they will respond to such an environment overwhelmingly, regardless of their religious background.

Basic Principle

The care ministry is the extension of the Lead Pastor and Care Pastors should make every effort to connect church members to the pastor as they relate to them in ministry. We continue to say that Care Pastors do not *replace* the pastor they *represent* their pastor.

We suggest that care pastors always use a phrase such as, "*Pastor (So-and-so) wanted me to stop by and visit you/ call you/ etc.*" when connecting with members of the congregation. This is vitally important because we never want to create the impression that the pastor does not care. Care Pastors are there *because* the pastor cares.

Our goal is to let every person that calls our church home to know they are: Valued, accepted, loved, cared for, and have a clear sense of belonging.
They are not just names in a database.

Through creating flocks (family groups) that relate to each other under the leadership of a Care Pastor, healthy support groups can potentially also be formed. When there is a need in one family, the others can bind together and aid in a Christ-like manner.

Living in community, and caring for each other, results in a healthy church — and the only way a church can grow is by being healthy. This is what made the early church become so powerful and influential. We seem to have missed this vital key in most of our churches today.

Five Points of Contact
Care Pastors should commit to staying in touch with their assigned families regularly. Our concept proposes five definite points of contact which are crucial to the successful outcome of a care ministry in any local church. Since it becomes the basic understanding of the entire ministry, Care Pastors must recognize and fully accept these points of contact. We will move slowly in covering these components to make sure the precepts are clear and easy to implement.

The following are the *five points of contact* we are taking into consideration:
1. Personal Contact
2. Sunday Connection
3. Monthly Contact
4. Celebrative Connection
5. Fifth Sunday Fellowship

Personal Contact
The first and foremost contact that should be made is referred to as *Personal Contact*. Of all the connections, this is the most crucial. The main purpose of this interaction is simply to become acquainted with someone you do not know, or to build closer ties with those you may already be familiar with.

Some find this the most exciting part of the entire concept. If it depended on them, that's all they would want to do. They can't wait to get with their people. To some other Care Pastors, on the other hand, this could be the most difficult and the most challenging part of the ministry. But if approached with the correct attitude and an unpretentious spirit, it can potentially be the most exciting and rewarding for them also.

What is very important to continually remember is the importance of this contact. It cannot be disregarded or even downplayed. It sets the scene for all future ministry and if not done, or conducted in a shabby way, will detrimentally affect the ongoing relationship. It will prove to be very discouraging to the Care Pastor and may eventually lead to failure. If done appropriately, it will establish a long-term relationship which will develop into healthy trust — a most important element.

Your first acquaintance with the family you are serving in this relationship should be by means of a personal, one-on-one, eye-to-eye contact. There is just no other more effective way to do so. Looking the person in the eye and visiting in a personal, congenial way opens the door to the relationship that will otherwise take a very long time to foster — if ever. There are various ways of accomplishing this aspect of ministry and we will introduce you to different means that have proven to be very successful.

Home Visit

While we realize there are numerous challenges to this approach, we still hold to the truth that the most effective way of establishing sound relationships is by means of a personal visit to someone's home. It is simply a fact that you can never learn so much of a person, so quickly, as a visit to their home. But please bear in mind that this personal contact is not meant to take place on a regular basis. It is normally a singular occurrence.

Learning about people by means of a visit to their home has nothing to do with how appealing or unappealing a home may be, how kept or unkempt it may be, or even what their furniture looks like. It has nothing to do with those things. It's about learning something about the people you may never have caught in any other way.

Perhaps this could be best illustrated by citing the first visit of a Care Pastor couple to an unfamiliar family.

After they had set up an appointment to see the couple, they arrived at the prescribed time. They were greeted very friendly at the door and then guided to the family room. The husband suggested where they should sit and made himself comfortable in his own recliner. His wife too sat in her favorite chair.

As the Care Pastor couple sat down, the wife noticed a picture of a young man in military uniform on the coffee table. It was obvious that this picture had some significance.

"Is this picture of the young man related to you?" She carefully asked with a gentle smile.

"Yes," the lady said, "that is a picture of our son that was killed in Afghanistan". It was impossible to miss the pain in her voice as she said it.

"Oh, I am so sorry to hear that. It could not have been easy, I am sure."

"No, no, it was definitely not easy," the husband now pitched in, "it was the hardest thing of our lives, and we are still not over the shock of it all."

The wife became somewhat emotional at this point and silently wiped a tear from her cheek. The Care Pastor continued by compassionately asking, "how old was he?"
"He was only twenty years old," the father said.
"Do you know what happened? Did they tell you how he died?"

Let me quickly interrupt the flow of the story by saying many people at this point will steer away from the subject and try to change the subject — not wanting to cause sorrow to the couple. But let me help you on this: People *want to* talk about the loved one they have lost. They want to share their heartache. Ignoring it will cause unbelievable pain. Having shown interest in the picture and asking what had happened to their son was the most genuine way of connecting with them. Let's get back to the story:

"Well, they told us as much as they knew at that time, which was not very comforting," the father said with a deep sigh.

Slowly, but surely, they shared the details they had received. Painfully he described what the Chaplain conveyed to them and went on to say how his wife woke up that morning, missing her son badly. She said that she could not wait to see him and secretly wondered if he may not surprise them with an unannounced visit. "She just felt something tugging deep down on her inside concerning our boy."

"So, when the doorbell rang, she knew it was him. She knew it was her son!" His lip began to quiver as he lowered his head. We both rushed to the front door with great anticipation, only to see the Chaplain standing there, and not our son. My wife looked at me and words were unnecessary. She fell into my arms and began to cry bitterly. She knew what that meant."

"May I please come in?" the Chaplain asked politely.

"Yes, sure, yes please come in."

"The Chaplain came in and sat on the sofa. My head was spinning like a top. I could literally feel the blood drain out of my head," the father said.

"Mr. and Mrs. Sanders, (not their real name) I am sorry that I have to bring you some bad news today," the Chaplain started.

"My wife began to cry hysterically. I couldn't honestly remember all he said. I lowered my head into my cupped hands and all I could think of was my son. His life replayed before my eyes as if someone had turned on a video," the father said, obviously very emotional. "It felt as though my heart was going to explode. It felt as though our world had come to an end."

"I am so sorry, so terribly sorry you had to go through this,", the Care Pastor said. "Were they able to tell you the exact date your son died?"

"Yes, it was on October 15, 2012." (Not the real date)

"And all along I thought our son was going to surprise us," the mother said, "that's what I felt all day long. How wrong I was!" Pain was still shallow in her emotions.

"If I may ask, what was his name?"

"Charles," the father said. "His name was Charles. We called him Charlie."

The mother added, "And he was all we had. All!" There was a moment of silence as she discreetly slipped her hand under that of her husband. By this time, the Care Pastor couple even became emotional too. (You can't help to feel the pain of people in their suffering. That's why we need people who care.)

The couple continued to share their feelings and later even started sharing some humoristic stories of their son. The atmosphere lightened, and the father said, "Oh, we're so sorry. We didn't mean to load our burdens on you!"

"Oh no," the Care Pastor said, "we're so glad you told us. We would never have known."

The rest of the visit went very cordial and pleasant. It ended with all four sharing delightful stories while they were sipping hot cider and enjoying ginger cookies. A classic example of effective care ministry.

Observation

There are a few things in this visit that I want to highlight for your attention:
- The *first* thing I want you to take note of is this: The moment the couple responded to the question of the picture on the coffee table and related their pain to the Care Pastors, they instantaneously *connected* with each other. They became friends. This is exactly what we are attempting to do — hopefully not always through tragedies.

- The *second* point I want you take note of is that while the Care Pastor was leading the conversation, his wife was carefully taking notes of certain things that were said; e.g. the young man's name, the date of the tragedy, his birthday, etc. (Somewhere during the conversation, she asked permission to jot down some notes.)
- The *third* thing I want you to notice is the importance of two people making the visit together. One person cannot lead the conversation and take notes at the same time — it will make him/her look like a reporter.
- The *fourth* important element to note is that the Care Pastors may never have known about this heart-rending occurrence in the couple's lives if they had not made this home visit.
- The *fifth* striking observation I want to highlight is the vital follow-up that flowed out of this visit. On the anniversary date of their son's death, the Care Pastor made a personal call to the parent's home. After Jim answered the phone the Care Pastor said,

"Hi Jim, this is Eddy. How are you doing?"
"Oh well, I guess we're doing fine. As good as we could, I guess."
"I understand," Eddy said. "That's why I'm calling, Jim. Pastor Shepherd wanted us to call to let you know that we remember that this is the day that Charlie died. We care about you."
There was a moment of silence before Jim responded.
"Wow, Ed, I had no idea you would remember. Yes... uh

"… yes … it's still tough," he said with emotion clearly to be heard in his voice.

"Jim, on behalf of all of us here at Caring Place Church we want you to know that we are praying that you will sense the comfort of the Comforter. May God strengthen you and Lucille today and every day. And please know, we will always be there for you."

"Thanks, Ed. Thank you very much. When I saw it was you calling, I turned on the speaker of my phone. Lucille is so blessed because of your love and care. Thanks, my friend! We'll never forget this. Also thank pastor for us, will you?"

"I certainly will, Jim. But before I let you go, is it okay if I pray a short prayer with you and Lucille over the phone?"

Now, imagine with me the effects it will have if this happens all over the church on a regular basis: Care Pastors calling heartbroken people on the anniversary date of the death of a spouse, a parent, a child, or some other loved one. Can you even conceive of what that will do in terms of bonding people with genuine love and concern? This step on its own will make a huge difference in the congregation and is worth all the effort of releasing people to care one for another. I know of no other churches doing this.

Facing Present-day Reality

Despite all the great advantages of a home visit, and regardless of how important such a connection may be, we fully realize that it may not always be feasible in all cases. Many people these days prefer that no one comes to their home. And there are many different reasons for this. It, therefore, necessitates us to look for acceptable and practical alternative options to make this important contact.

While there is really no substitute for a personal home visit, the next best alternative may be to instead invite them to come to your home. Now, if you don't want people to come to your home... well, Houston, then we have a problem! Just kidding. While this may be a viable option — and in some places, it may still work — reality lets us know that less people will be willing to go to a stranger's home than even having someone come to their home.

So, let's look at some practical solutions to overcome these obstacles. Here are some ideas to stimulate your thinking and help you find feasible ways to make this contact happen:

- Meet in a restaurant or coffee shop somewhere within reach of all involved.
- Many churches these days have cafes or coffee shops in the foyer. This is a great place to meet before or after church.
- Another practical suggestion (where a church is not outfitted with a coffee shop) is to simply arrange a meeting with them briefly before or after church somewhere in the church building. Remember, you only need a few minutes.

These are practical steps that are very workable, especially if you see here below how simple this contact really is. None of these alternatives provide the incredible benefits of a home visit, but it does at least create a means for becoming acquainted, which at the end of the day is what this personal contact is really all about.

An interesting observation we have found is that many Care Pastors who could initially not succeed in arranging an initial home visit, later, as the relationship developed, indeed were able to visit their families in their respective homes.

As we discuss these connections, and especially their implementation, it may be helpful if we remind ourselves that our entire ministry effort has a long-term goal and is not intended to span only over a month or two. If something doesn't happen initially, time may be your best friend.

The Purpose of the Personal Contact
1. To basically become acquainted (putting names and faces together) with each of your family groups.
2. To explain to them what the *Care Ministry* is all about (using the care ministry definition found in Chapter Three).
3. To explain how care will be provided by clarifying expectation of this ministry (using C.A.R.E. as an acronym). See Chapter Five.
4. To make sure you have all their correct contact and personal information (birthdays, anniversary, etc.), and provide them with yours (a printed business card provided by the church is most helpful).
5. To spend a few moments in prayer with them before you leave.
6. To provide them with your personal contact information.

It's Not Cold Turkey
A very reassuring part in the process of making your personal contact is that you will not be connecting with anyone "cold turkey."

They will already have been informed about the *Care Ministry Network* through official church newsletters, other communications, or the new members conference. They will furthermore also have received a personal letter from the church office notifying them that you will be their Care Pastor, and that you would be connecting with them shortly. So, basically, they're expecting this contact!

Now, this makes it much easier for you! But at the same time, bear in mind that it also places a huge responsibility on your shoulders. Since they already now know about you, and know you are going to contact them, and then you don't, it will leave a seriously bad impression on both you, and the care ministry — even the church. So, seize the opportunity and meet new friends. (We have built these principles into the system to make the concept organic).

The Anatomy of a Visit

Since the personal contact is decisive for setting the pace for developing futuristic relationships between Care Pastors and their flocks, it will serve us well to spend some time in discussing the best ways to make the contact effective. We encourage Care Pastors to make this contact within six weeks after they have been commissioned.

Assuming a visit to your family groups' home is your choice of making the personal contact, we suggest the following helpful points as you prepare to make this connection:

1. Preparation for the Visit

The first visit is especially important and will essentially be different from all future contacts. It will set the platform for ongoing ministry opportunities and relational development.

1.1. Call ahead. Your first action step is to call ahead and make an appointment for your visit. Never just show up at someone's home. Be very kind, courteous, and friendly as you communicate to whomever answers the call.

- Ask them if this is a good time to talk — it greatly helps the flow of the conversation when you are sensitive to their time.
- After a brief, general, chit-chat (very brief), state the purpose of your call — which is to set up an appointment for your first visit.
- Ask them if they have received a letter from the church notifying them of your intention to contact them. (Respond accordingly.)
- Tell them the main purpose of your visit is to meet them personally, and furthermore to inform them more about the purpose and function of the Care Ministry.
- Assure them that your visit will be brief.
- When requesting the appointment, it always helps to suggest a date rather than asking them when a good time will be. E.g., "I have Tuesday or Thursday evening at seven available; which of these will work best for you?"
- Be sure to make a note of the date and confirm it before you pray a short prayer over the phone.

1.2. Preparation in Prayer: Pray before you leave your home — not in front of the person's house. Ask the Holy Spirit to give you wisdom and confidence as you make the visit.

1.3 Check your material: Make sure you have all the relevant forms, cards, brochures, etc., with you. (Don't forget your pen!) Of course, if you're using electronics you will have it all together.

1.4. Information: Make sure you have their correct address and the directions to get there. It's always helpful to keep their telephone number handy — just in case you must call for some reason on your way there.

1.5. Be on Time: Make sure you arrive on time. If you are not five minutes early for your appointment, you are late! (Don't be too early either!) If you're meeting them in a coffee shop, church café, or somewhere else, be looking out for them. (Don't be hiding behind your phone or tablet!)

2. The Visit Itself

2.1. Introduction: Introduce yourself, especially if you have not met them before. (You may be nervous but do remember to smile!)

2.2. Politeness: If making a home visit, wait to be invited in, and don't just rush to the first open chair either. Be sensitive — you don't want to take their favorite chair (it's their comfort zone). Let your hosts suggest a good place for you to be seated.

If meeting them at a café or coffee shop, or somewhere else, suggest some comfortable seats for them, and let them be seated first.

3.2. Alertness: Carefully look for "conversation starters" such as pictures, hobbies, keepsakes, in a home, or talk about something like the weather if not in a home. Pay special attention to children where applicable — it will win the game for you! Be on the alert for possible physical restrictions someone in the family may have or whatever other circumstances may influence your connection as you meet with your flock family.

4. The Conversation

Not everyone finds it easy to engage in a conversation with people they have never met before. The greatest fear is usually not knowing how to get started and even more so, what to talk about. Usually, once the conversation gets going, it's much easier.

Jesus foresaw the anxiety level of His disciples as He sent them out to talk with people. He assured them with these words: "Do not be anxious how you are to speak or what you are to say, for what you are to say will be given you in that hour" (Matthew 10:19).

Jesus' assurance is to you as well as to the twelve, for He said, "Lo, I am with you always, even to the close of the age" (Matthew 28:20).

We suggest you use the acrostic **F.O.R.M.** as a helpful tool to get started with a conversation, whether you make a home visit or meet with your family groups at some other location. Many people have found this method most useful to carry on a mutually productive and pleasant discussion:

F – Family. People, for the most part, love talking about themselves. It's less threatening and therefore the easiest way to connect. So, start there. Especially if you do not know the family, you may want to ask conversation-starting questions such as, "Is (our city) home to you?" "How long have you been living here?" Where did you live before coming here?" Which city do you prefer?" Carefully and kindly inquire about their children, parents, relatives, or whatever is applicable. Should you be in their home, look for displayed pictures, extraordinary keepsakes, antique furniture, etc. These make excellent conversation starters.

O – Occupation. Simply shift the conversation to enquiring about his/her occupation. Asking about a person's livelihood is a way of showing interest in them. Feel free to ask them where they work, or what they do — but be sensible and do not let it sound as though you are probing. Try to make your conversation flow naturally. Bear in mind, they may be just as nervous as you are. So, relax and confidently lead the way.

R – Recreation. Ask them if they have any hobbies, sports, or any forms of recreation. Show great interest in what they're interested in but allow them to do the talking. If their team is not your favorite team, let them win this game!

Under "R" you can also talk about "Religious" matters such as asking questions about past and present church involvement. You could refer to the pastor's most recent sermon — (never ask if they can remember what the pastor preached about!) and make some positive comment. This is an appropriate time to talk about current exciting events in the church. Also share what God is doing in your life presently — but keep it short!

M – Message. By "message" we simply mean moving into the reason of your visit or contact (see below). Clarifying the motive for this relationship will ensure a healthy ongoing development for the future.

Take a few moments to explain that the reason for your visit is:
1. To get better acquainted, "We just wanted to meet you in person, so you can at least see what we look like and we can also put your names and faces together.")
2. To explain **how** the Care Ministry Network functions (use the definition).
3. To explain **what** they can expect from the relationship (using the "C.A.R.E." concept outline):

"The way we would like to develop a ministry relationship with you is through the following quick and easy steps":
- "We would love **to stay in** *contact* with you on a regular basis without 'policing' you or becoming overburdening. We just want you to know that we care and that you are important to us.
- "In order for us to stay in touch with you, **I (we) will be** *available* to you whenever you need us and will at all times make ourselves as visible as possible at church. Here is our card with all our contact information. You can call us at any time."
- "Another reason why we wanted to meet with you is to let you know that **we will** *remember to pray* **for you** regularly and will count it an honor if you would let us know when there are specific matters you want us to pray about."
- "To help you in your spiritual growth I (we) will endeavor to be **a good** *example* to you in every respect and help you become everything God desires for you."

This kind of friendly conversation establishes confidence and begins to build the relationship. Make sure you stay on point and do not make the visit too long. Let them long for more fellowship rather than wishing for it to end.

4. Important Points Concerning the Visit

This first visit should be very cordial and put your new-found friends at ease. Your ultimate purpose should be to contact this family (or individual) and ensure that ongoing relationship will continue.

4.1. Pray before departing

Be sure to ask them, "Before we each go our separate ways, what is there in particular you would like me to pray with you about?" Pray with them (him/her) and commit to continue to do so.

Paying close attention to their prayer request may very well be the key that opens the door to building a strong relationship.

4.2. Departure

Depart graciously. Express your appreciation to them for giving you quality time. Build a bridge for future contact. The way you exit the conversation will be the way you will enter the next time. Assure them that you will be looking out for them at church events and that they should feel free to connect with you also.

4.3. Alertness and sensitivity

Take careful note of their interests, hobbies, activities, needs, family situation, spiritual state, etc. Check your records and make sure you have their correct, pertinent information — address, dates of birth/ anniversary/ names of children, etc.

5. Log the visit

The information you record will be helpful tools as you build future relationships. It will also serve as a reminder to you of their personal whereabouts to contact them on important days.

- Record their place of employment, school, hobbies, and other interests.
- Make notes of all you can remember. It is always most helpful when there are two people making this contact together.
- Make out the first visit report and submit it according to the instructions given by your Leadership Team. This is sometimes an unpleasant task to some people, but it is crucial to the ongoing success of this ministry. This is many times where character comes in to play.
- If we do not retain our accountability, we will soon lose interest in what we are doing. There is truly enormous value in retaining our responsibility. As the saying goes: people do not do what is *expected;* they only do what is *inspected.*

You should develop your own personal binder (hardcopy or electronic) with all the personal information of your families. It will become a very handy ready reference tool as you continue to build relationships.

By being alert on your first contact, you can gain insight into . . .
- Family members not present
- Crises—past, present, or future

- Special events/days coming up
- Sickness or other needs
- Moods, relationships, attitudes
- Work situations
- Spiritual interests or needs

All these observations are valuable to incorporate into your future contacts. Your time spent in prayer, talking with God about your pastoral observations, will generate creative contact ideas over the next months and even years. These are the things that make you sensitive to the needs of your families, create opportunity for ministry and become a catalyst for building endearing relationship. You cannot help but love the people you continuously pray for with Christ-like passion.

7

THE SUNDAY CONNECTION

The second *Point of Contact* in our caring process is known as the *Sunday Connection*.

Most Care Pastors do not only find the *Sunday Connection* to be one of the easiest steps, but also agree that it is one of the most invigorating of all the connections we make. It doesn't take long for this connection to catch on in the entire congregation.

For the *Sunday* Connection to occur Care Pastors connect with each of their families every Sunday in a meaningful way. But before you freak out, it's not as challenging as it sounds. This contact does not necessarily have to be by means of a conversation or a handshake. It can instead be done by something as simple as a nod, a thumbs-up, a wave of the hand, a fist bump, or some other means of connection. What is important, however, is that *you make eye contact* with the person.

The effectiveness of this connection lies in the fact that when a Care Pastor transfers a signal to one of his/her flock members, and the member responds, *connection* has been made. Actual communication has taken place even if it be non-verbal communication. The members now know the Care Pastor knows they are in attendance, while the Care Pastor knows the members know they have been noticed.

This in return conveys the message to the members that they are important enough for the Care Pastor to take time to look out for them and connect with them. This action conveys to each member the important message that they belong and are accepted as being part of the congregation.

You will be surprised to know how many spouses check with each other after church to see whether their Care Pastor looked them up. Very often, on the other hand, Care Pastors have reported that their flock members have begun to look them up instead and were looking forward to their connection.

Although we said that the *Sunday Connection* is simply a distant communication, it will serve the Care Pastors well to have a face-to-face conversation with each flock member from time-to-time. In smaller churches it has become customary for Care Pastors and members to have a conversation instead of a simple gesture across the room. Regardless of how the connection is made, the bottom-line value of it is the rightful reason to reach out to others with purpose.

NOTE: To avoid church members get the feeling of *big brother* watching them, when you connect with your families each Sunday, function under the *proverbial radar*. Make your engagement seem natural and avoid being too obvious. Making eye contact and receiving some response should be your object. The functioning of the *connection* should be a "secret action" mainly understood only by the Care Pastors. It should not be announced from the pulpit.

Follow the Steps

Whenever you have connected with each family (not necessarily each member of the family) your responsibility is fulfilled and unless there is something to follow up on, there is nothing more to do until next Sunday. There are times when some action is required from your side and we will highlight some of these here below:

When you don't find them

In cases where you are seemingly not able to connect with a particular family unit on a given Sunday (or whenever you gather), your appropriate action will be to call them immediately after the service. The purpose of this call again is not to "police" them but instead to determine whether they may be experiencing any challenges, illness, or crisis of some sorts that you may assist them with.

"Hi, Joe, this is John," the Care Pastor said over the phone, "Trust you are doing great?"

"Hey, John. We're doing wonderful!"

"Joe, I'm just calling to see if you guys are okay. I know our church is growing pretty fast, but I didn't see you in church this morning."

"Oh man, thanks for calling, John. I meant to call you, but we have been quite busy. Mary's family came in unexpectedly and we hadn't seen them in the longest time. They weren't prepared to go to church so we decided to camp around the pool today."

The loud noise in the background let you know they were having fun.

"Oh, that's fine, Joe. Just wanted to make sure everything is fine."

"Sure, John, we are just fine. And tell Pastor Shepherd we'll be back next Sunday."

"Great, Joe. Tell Mary 'Hi' for us and have fun! See you next Sunday."

You can only imagine the many benefits of a connection such as this. This is the glue that keeps it all together and makes sure people are not falling through the cracks. The worst thing John could have done was to simply hope Jim and his family would be back the following Sunday and do nothing else.

So, in this case there was no apparent crisis, and the Care Pastor simply had to report the outcome to their upline.

At times, it could be different. If you call and cannot reach them, keep calling until you get a response. If you have their mobile phone, send them a kind text. If you cannot reach them, do not let go. Contact your Care Shepherd and determine appropriate action. If necessary, and possible, go to their home. You may never know what's going on. The word of wisdom here is: use common sense and rely upon the Holy Spirit.

Follow through with any needs that may arise. Inform your Care Shepherd if there is an apparent emergency that needs attention.

Facing a Crisis

Now, what if John called, and instead of Joe joyfully relating their family gathering, he said,

"John, thank you so much for calling. I have been threatening to call you the whole morning, but, my friend, I am running around like a chicken with its head cut off!"

"What's going on, Joe? How can we help?"

"Man, they rushed Mary to the hospital and she's not doing well. She may have to stay there for a while." You could hear the anxiety in his voice.

"And I have these two little kids of ours running around all over. I have to try and feed them, clothe them, and heaven alone knows how I'm going to get them to school tomorrow."

"You said Mary is in the hospital?" Which hospital is she in?

"She's in the Get Well Soon Hospital."

"Joe, will it be okay for us to go and see her? (Always ask permission).

"Sure, John. She's in room number 1023."

"We will go as soon as possible. But, Joe, talk to me about the children. I can possibly find someone who may be able to help?

Note the Follow-through Action

His first action step is to report the situation to his Care Shepherd. He then calls the other families in his flock and shares with them the challenges Jim and his family are facing (not giving all the finer details). He requests these families to pray for Joe and Mary.

When applicable, John then asks these families to assist Jim in whichever way they possibly can. Some may provide meals, others offer to look after the kids, others are willing to help get them to school, and the list goes on.

In this way, the help is not left to an overworked committee at the church but is shared among a few families. The good news for the Care Pastor is, however, that in all reality this does not happen every week or even every month. In most cases it's a rare occurrence, but it provides a wonderful network when crisis do show up.

You may ask, "does it work?" "Do churches ever really apply this?" Pastor D from Florida will tell you, "*when that mammoth crisis hit our church, it was the Care Pastors who stepped in to connect with the families and to facilitate them to help each other. If it weren't for them, we would not have made it.*"

Larry, a Care Director, will tell you, "*It has ignited a fire of passion among our people. I know it may sound funny, but it's like some of them can't wait for someone to face a challenge. They just want to help!*"

Several others will tell you the same thing. It's amazing, so amazing, to see how people pick up their responsibilities and serve one another. People are desperate to feel valuable in their churches; they need to be needed. But if there's nothing to commit to, they will soon be on their way somewhere else.

In case of death

Should your connection reveal a death of a loved one in the family, we suggest you follow the following steps:
- Call your Care Shepherd immediately.
- If you cannot reach your Care Shepherd, call the Lead Pastor, or one of the other ministers immediately (it has now moved from congregational care to crisis care).
- Call the other families in your flock for prayer.
- Get to the family as soon as possible (your presence is still important).

- Make yourself available and help wherever needed.
- Involve other flock families where possible to assist the bereaving family.
- Attend the *visitation* whenever possible.
- Attend the funeral (if possible) and be sure to connect with the family at the service.
- Give special attention to the family (or individual) after the funeral. This is when it's most needed. Prayer is always welcome. If your pastor is not the one officiating, convey his/her condolences to the family.
- Make a note of the date — so you can call on the anniversary date and let them know, "Pastor (Shepherd) wanted me to call to let you know that we remember this day. We are praying that you will sense the comfort of the Comforter..."

Summary

Times of Crisis

When people face crisis in their lives it creates precious opportunities for reaching out to them in love, building relationship and showing them that you, the pastor, and the church, really care about them. This is the time to be *"love with skin on."*

If one of them should be in the hospital, be sure to visit them as soon as possible and follow up on a consistent basis — and **inform** your Care Shepherd and the church office about this. Always check with the family that your visit to the hospital is appropriate, and which times would be best.

Involving Other Flock Members

Crisis moments also create great ministry opportunity for the rest of your flock member families to show love and concern by taking care of meals, small children and daily chores where and when needed. (For instance, when a mother is hospitalized, and the need exist).

In times of death, great concern and care should be extended with the added opportunity of also helping before, during, and after the funeral service. Arrange with flock members to be available for diverse kinds of needs that may develop.

Special attention in the days **following** the funeral service is crucial! This is the time when people who have lost a loved one face their greatest crisis. There are usually many family members and friends that surround the hurting family (or individual) through the funeral, but normally leave and get on with their own lives when the formalities are over.

As a Care Pastor, be sure to be available and offer your prayer and spiritual support as best you can. Just "being there for them" is all that's needed in many cases. The more serious the crisis, the more the need for follow-up, and the more time it will require walking with them. But the rewards that come out of this kind of relationship are priceless.

Whenever any other emergency befalls a family the Care Pastor should respond appropriately. It is during times of crisis that actual ministry takes place and provides great fulfillment to Care Pastors. Always keep your Care Shepherd posted on the development of any emergency.

Times of need when care could be given:
- ✓ Illness
- ✓ Death in family

- ✓ Hospitalization
- ✓ Moving
- ✓ Divorce/Separation
- ✓ Change of job
- ✓ Lack of transport
- ✓ Accident
- ✓ Disability
- ✓ Disaster
- ✓ Chemical dependency
- ✓ Legal problems
- ✓ Depression
- ✓ Church problem
- ✓ Trouble with neighbors

Helpful Observations

The *Sunday Connection* is quite possibly the most important step in the process when it comes to spanning a net under people, so no one falls through the cracks, and the most effective way of avoiding people slip through the back door. This connection is certainly important for building relationships and developing accountability, but also becomes potential indicators of people's seeming behavior. An observant Care Pastor will notice these things if these patterns are understood.

Since many churches may not necessarily be aware of the signals members unknowingly send when they get ready to leave a church, we will touch on some of these indicators briefly. It may be most helpful to know these, so we can avoid people slipping away. and do not have a ministry plan for reaching out to these people. While we again want to caution against being a *Big Brother/Sister,* we do want to suggest that, in your process of looking out for the flock, you be aware of some of the following:

Seating

Most of us are creatures of habits and sit in the same seat every Sunday — which is both good and bad. It is helpful to the Care Pastor in as much as it makes it easier to *find* flock members each Sunday. But it could also become an identification of potential unrest the members are facing. For instance, people who usually sit closer to the front of the church, and suddenly begin to gradually sit further and further to the back, or closer to a door, are inadvertently indicating that they are on their way out.

Others who change from the area where they normally sit, could potentially be signifying they want to estrange themselves from the people who know them well, so they would not be easily missed once they slip away.

Absenteeism

When faithful people increasingly begin to miss the services, they may very well unintentionally be sending the message that they are dissatisfied with something, or even worse, are church-shopping.

Ministry Involvement

Another possible indicator may be when members begin to drop out of their involvement in ministry and their commitment lessens. They usually say they need a break, or that their season for ministry is changing, or that they are burnt out, or at times blame it on their children — and the list goes on. While some of these reasons may be valid, a Care Pastor should not ignore the potential of them secretly seeking *the back door.* The truth is that people sometimes feel they have to leave their church before they will be released from overburdening responsibilities that have been placed on them over the years. Be sensitive to this scenario.

> People usually disengage
> Before they disappear

Action Steps

When you observe some of these signs, the following may be helpful:
- Inform your Care Shepherd of your observations to gain support and determine appropriate action (refer to your pastor if the Care Shepherd level is not in place).
- Stay in touch with the family as closely as they would allow you.
- Continue to pray for them.
- A "Thinking of You" card may also be appropriate — but be perceptive.
- Stay on the alert, be available, and maintain contact.

Stages of Disaffiliating
- The discomfort stage.
- The withdrawing stage.
- The exiting stage.

We do not intend to deal with these stages in-depth but want to at least have Care Pastors be aware of these, so they can be helpful to avoid church members fall through the cracks.

The Discomfort Stage

It almost seems as though most, if not all, people find them in this stage at some point in time. If detected in good time the problem can usually be resolved easily. It usually occurs when people become disenchanted with something that is happening or has happened in the congregation, they feel uncomfortable with.

It could relate to things such as change in worship style, change of service times, length of service, change of meeting rooms, or any such matters. It could of course relate to many other similar things. I have often referred to it as "people having a pebble in their shoe" indicating that they continue walking but every step is accompanied by anxiety.

If ignored, it may potentially become a problem, but if detected early on, can usually be resolved by simply allowing them to express their feelings and giving them the opportunity to air their grievances or ask their questions. Once heard, people oftentimes feel better and regain their energy. At times the input of a Care Shepherd or reference to the Lead Pastor will be necessary.

The value of the care ministry as a whole comes into play when these situations arise. Too often we hope people will *get over it* — and many times they do. But very often they unfortunately don't. If it doesn't result in them leaving the church, it usually, at minimum, causes them to slow down and decrease in ministry activity, sadly with apathy as a result.

Simply paying attention to people, letting them know they matter, and that their opinions count, satisfies most unhappy members. I have found that giving people the opportunity to share their feelings and merely listening to them lovingly in the *discomfort stage,* resolves ninety percent of their grievances.

The Withdrawal Stage

Church members who do not have their dissatisfactions settled usually move into *The Withdrawal Stage*. They are obviously not happy and for the most part show it in their attitudes. They tend to also withdraw from ministry and are inclined to move their seating position in the church further back to the rear of the church. It is unfortunately true that their attitudes are often also reflected in their financial support of the church.

Since this stage begins to move outside of our recommendation of basic congregational care, and the responsibility of a Care Pastor, the credentialed pastoral staff should handle members who clearly indicate withdrawal.

The Exiting Stage

This stage belongs to the attention of the Lead Pastor. Every church should have a set exit strategy in place. This enables pastors and exiting members to separate in a Christ-like manner, which brings glory to God and respect to the church. If done with the correct attitude and in a Christian-professional way, I have found many once disgruntled members to later return to the congregation with a much better attitude than before. Our attitude should be, "We are not losing people, we are "sowing" them into another congregation."

CONCLUSION

Do not see your connection with your people as a mere obligation. Instead, be very sensitive to the leadership of the Holy Spirit as you connect with your people with purpose. It is often just your availability by means of eye-contact that gives them the liberty to share a burden they are undergoing. If left untouched, they may go home with the same load upon their shoulders. After all, it IS all about "loving your neighbor as you love yourself!" You may never know what your *Connection* could mean to a discouraged brother or sister. Let your service to the body of Christ remain a ministry of love and care — no more and no less.

8

FURTHER CONTACTS

In this chapter, we are going to discuss the final three *Points of Contact* in our caring process. Each of them is described in a way whereby it will make it easily understood and simple to implement. Each step of the process has its own purpose and helps us complete the process of congregational care.

There is an obvious possibility that when we consider all the suggested contacts within one glimpse, it may seem overwhelming to a potential Care Pastor. Bear in mind however, that your first contact happens only once, your Sunday connection, once a week, and obviously your monthly connection (explained here below) occurs only once a month. The first two take somewhat more involvement than the final three. The further we proceed, the less cumbersome the steps become.

Also remember, you are only responsible for five units (families or individuals) and they do not all face a crisis every week or even every month. Furthermore, since our concept requires that care should be provided by a team of two people, the tasks can be equally divided among them, which makes the obligation even easier.

As your care system develops, you will also at some point have an assistant care-pastor-couple in place, which means you then have four people among whom the duties can be divided. One person alone should never be making all these contacts and connections on their own. That's not the way this system was designed. Spread the duties among all, as long as there is one in your team who takes the lead.

Monthly Contact

The *third contact* in our sequence is known as the *Monthly Contact* and becomes the bedrock of your ministry. This is the one step you just cannot neglect. When we discussed the *C.A.R.E. Module* in chapter 5, I stated that one of the responsibilities of a Care Pastor is to make monthly contacts with each of their families. The way we achieve that contact is what we are dealing with in this segment.

You should make a direct and "personal contact" with each family in your flock only once a month. More than that will become overwhelming, unless they are experiencing a crisis.

The purpose of this ongoing contact is to stay in touch with each family and to maintain a healthy relationship.

Since this is a direct (personal) contact, it becomes the most powerful way through which the church expresses to each household that they are indeed part of the church family and are genuinely valued. When a church does not have this level of care, most members never receive any form of affirmation. Keeping these channels open also provides a wholesome atmosphere in the congregation.

You are not required to speak with *each* member of a family — as long as you have reasonably connected with an adult in the household, you have fulfilled your obligation.

Phone Call

This monthly contact cannot and should not be made by means of an email, a text message, or even a card or note of some kind. A personal, purposeful phone call is what we are saying. It should never be a lengthy conversation, but should be focused, very cordial and certainly encouraging. We will say more in just a moment. Some Care Pastors prefer to make this another home visit, which is fine, but it is not expected.

Unless someone had a birthday or other form of celebration, or faced a crisis during the month, you have had no verbal communication with your people. This reality increases the importance of making this contact. People need to know that someone is aware of their existence and cares about them. People often say, "We look forward to the call of our Care Pastors. It's always exciting and encouraging. When we hear from them, we feel part of the family."

It is two-way communication

This monthly contact serves as a two-way communication. *Firstly*, from the Care Pastor, showing sincere care and love for the family, and *secondly*, an opportunity for each family to share their testimonies, concerns, questions, prayer requests or whatever may be on their minds, with the Care Pastor. It builds a strong bond and develops sound relationships. That's why constant contact is imperative.

Annual Prayer Visit

I know of some churches where the Care Pastors take one of their monthly contacts per *year* and turn it into a Prayer Visit in their people's homes. This, I believe, is very powerful and needs serious consideration. I mention this as a suggestion though, not necessarily an expectation.

The results have proven to be so dynamic that I am mentioning it here as a recommendation, even if you do not implement this procedure during the first year.

The following points capsulate the purpose of the monthly contact:
1. Basically, staying in touch with your flock to maintain the caring relationship
2. Enquire about their well-being
3. Answer any questions they may have regarding the church, a ministry, or whatever the case may be
4. Inform them of upcoming events, church news, available ministry opportunities, etc.
5. PRAY with them specifically.

Some guidelines

We do not want to make the *Monthly Contact* superfluous. It should truly be intended to add value to the family (individual) and to the relationship overall. In some cases, it may be appropriate to make an appointment with the family to set a specific time to call. You do not want to play "phone-tag." When setting up a call-appointment, assure them that you don't require a lot of time. When calling without a time-appointment, always ask them if it's a goodtime to talk when you connect with them on the phone.

Some added pointers may be helpful in developing your ongoing relationships with your families. The following added things may be included, although off-course not necessarily during every call:
- Be very sensitive to the needs of each family.
- Check on the correctness of their personal information and inform the church office of any changes.

- Thank them for their faithful support to the church and for being part of the church family.
- Give them an opportunity to ask questions or share some of their own thoughts.
- Impart some spiritual value to them — read an appropriate verse.
- Pray for them — and again ask, "Is there anything in particular that I can pray with you about?"
- Be alert for those who may need special attention and refer it to your Care Shepherd
- As you build relationships with your families by means of these calls, be attentive to recognize potential Care Pastors and recommend them to your Care Shepherd

Romans 1:11 says, "For I long to see you, that I may impart to you some spiritual gift, so that you may be established—" (NKJV)

After Your Contact
- Make notes of things you need to follow-up on.
- Fill out relevant Report Card (whether electronically or hard copy).
- Report your visit to your Care Shepherd — especially if there are some things that need his/her attention.
- Send a handwritten card, or even a text message to the family as follow-up.
- Reach out in prayer to the Lord on behalf of each family continually.

Celebrative Connection

The *Celebrative Connection* is the fourth step in our caring process and is usually associated with some celebration in the lives of your people. All people have times of merriment that provide great opportunities for suitable and welcomed contacts from their Care Pastor. It falls well within the Scripture expression that says, *"If one member is honored, all the members rejoice with it."*

The truth is, however, that most of our people rejoice by themselves, and nobody in the congregation is aware of their cheerful celebration. People graduate, get engaged, expect a baby, or receive a huge promotion, and nobody in the church celebrates with them. In this *Celebrative Connection,* we intend to change this *status quo.* We want the church family to join in the celebration. The following ideas may help us we consider opportunities

Birthdays

Birthdays are wonderful times of celebration, and all people have one! As a Care Pastor you should make a personal phone call to each member of their flock on the day of their birthday.

Say something like, "Pastor <*Faithful*> wanted me to call to say, 'Happy Birthday' on behalf of all of us. We are happy to have you as part of our church family. May God bless you with many more healthy and prosperous years to come!" (Never ask people how old they are!) Follow through with a short, but cordial conversation.

(We always say, "Pastor <*Faithful*> wanted me to call/ visit you/ etc." We are joining the hands of the leaders with those of the followers).

It is always a good idea to also mail a birthday card to each of them under your name, even if the church office would do the same.

Personal, hand-written notes and cards have once again become very popular. Electronic media has become generic in appearance. Break the mold! We all love to receive a "Happy Birthday" by means of an email, text, or on social media. But the feeling is quite different when someone sends you a personal birthday card in the mail. You realize that someone took the time and made a special effort to get that greeting to you. You know it took more than just hitting "send" on some electronic device. It's these small things that make people feel valued and accepted and makes a huge difference in people's lives. These connections develop strong bonds of relationships and build the kind of community that cannot easily be detached.

Thom S. Rainer mentions seven reason why handwritten notes will revolutionize your ministry activities:
1. It moves you to a spirit of gratitude.
2. It reminds you of the blessings God has given you.
3. It takes the focus off negativity in the church.
4. It is incredibly rewarding to the recipients.
5. It changes the ethos and culture of the church.
6. It improves personal relationships.
7. It (could) happen 365 times a year. (Parenthesis added).

Rainer on Leadership. Lifeway Christian Resources, Nashville, TN. 2018

Other Celebrations

In the process of building healthy relationships, Care Pastors usually stay close in touch with their flocks and readily pick up on all special occasions that occur or will occur within their people's lives. Many of these events are non-repetitive and therefore need our special attention — graduation, birth of a baby, receiving an award or scholarship, etc.

When these special events happen in your family groups, a phone call should be the least of your actions. Additionally, you may still want to send a card or some other appropriate message under your own name. Whenever possible, make every attempt to attend open-ceremonies, such as graduations, weddings, retirement party, etc. This is not mandatory, but your people will appreciate every act of kindness shown during times of celebration. It acknowledges their individuality and recognizes them as a person.

Note

When people have been assigned to you, the church office will usually provide you with all the available pertinent information of those you are responsible for — full names, birthdays, anniversary dates, address, phone numbers, email address, etc. When you make your first, personal contact, you should verify this information and adjust the data where necessary. It will furthermore be very helpful to the staff if you would inform the office of any discrepancies you found.

Times of Joy and Celebration that provide opportunities for connection:
- Marriage
- New home
- Graduation
- Ordination or other credentialing
- Promotion/election
- Anniversary

- Retirement
- Awards (of all kinds)
- Birth of a baby
- Adoption of a child
- Birthdays, etc.

Fifth Sunday Fellowship

The fifth and final point of contact in our caring process is known as the *Fifth Sunday Fellowship*. It is a proven fact that most individuals today long to build significant relationships. Modern times have made people become reclusive while the complexity of life has estranged them from each other. Friendships are just not so commonly formed anymore. That underscores the reason for authentic congregational care and fellowship. Those churches that build on this understanding will continue to be relevant and meet the needs of its members.

The *Fifth Sunday Fellowship* is held four times per year on the last Sunday of each month that has five Sundays. Depending on the circumstances, these fellowships could be held during the afternoon or early evening. This could potentially mean that the entire congregation will meet for fellowship on the same day at diverse places, four times a year.

The premise is for the Care Pastor to gather all the flock members (five family units) to a combined time of meaningful fellowship, fun, and recreation. This is not intended to be a time of Bible Study, intercessory prayer or even a teaching event. It's a time of *Koinonia* — true Christian fellowship.

Where?

- At the Care Pastors home
- At the home of one of the families

- At a restaurant, park, picnic grounds, bowling alley
- At the church
- Or wherever it is most practical

The main purpose of this gathering is to build relationships. The event is restricted only by the imagination and creativity of the Care Pastor. It should be a time of relaxation, friendship, and fun for all. Involve the families of your flock to give their suggestions for this event and help in the organization. Let them *buy* into to the occasion and have them feel it is *their* time. Do not, however, over-organize the affair!

Children should be included. Arrange activities for children where applicable — and once again, involve the parents in organizing the event. Don't do it all alone!

Opportunity. Not only is this a time for Care Pastors to get closer to their flocks, but also provides the opportunity for the families to get acquainted and the Care **Shepherds** to connect with the flocks. This creates a healthy atmosphere of love and care in the entire congregation.

Outreach. The *Fifth Sunday Fellowship* also creates an opportunity for church members to invite their friends and family to attend this social event. In this non-threatening environment, they will get to become acquainted with those in your *little flock* and feel less hesitant to attend church with you in the future. Be cautious, however, to not overwhelm them. Keep the emphasis on fellowship. Let them simply be exposed to a Christ-like environment. This is not a time to preach!

Alternatives. During a very interesting follow-up seminar I conducted at a church, that was effectively implementing the Care Ministry Network, they shared with me an interesting alternative of applying the all-church fellowship we suggest.

Instead of having their fellowships on the fifth Sunday of a month, they utilize already existing public holidays on the calendar for these events. They traditionally have all-church picnics and/or dinner on the grounds on Memorial Day, 4th of July, Labor Day, etc. The only change they made was to structure the day according to the care ministry expectation and found it to work wonderfully. Instead of families simply gathering on their own, they are now getting together as family groups with their Care Pastors. With busy schedules and full church programs it makes good sense to utilize those dates already slated.

We suggest fellowship on the fifth Sundays, but that is all it is — a suggestion. Any other days will work fine as long as you schedule some meaningful fellowship for the family-groups to meet with their Care Pastors and with each other.

Further advantages for these times of fellowship are that families get to meet people in the church they have never met before. This is important for many reasons:

- Some people are withdrawn and do not mix easily with others they don't know. Sunday services are not always conducive for developing meaningful relationships.
- Since we always tend to gather with the same people we already know, when we meet within our flock family groups, we of necessity get outside of our comfort zones and connect with people we have never met.
- It also helps families to put names and faces together at these fellowships, which is off-course most helpful in times when the Care Pastor calls upon them to help each other in times of crisis as described under the *Sunday Connection*.

The Care Ministry Network has at its core, meeting the needs of people and being *love with skin on* — and very effectively also includes both *relationship* and *fellowship*. It is not meant to be another ministry where people selectively choose to be part of but is rather the church reaching out to all its members. It's a powerful way of closing the back door of the church and making people feel secure, cherished, and taken care of. Churches may choose to develop their system as tight as they deem necessary or implement it in whatever way will fit their church's culture. Be careful, however, to not water it down to the point where it has little value.

9

SOME PRACTICAL LOGISTICS

We have assertively clarified the responsibilities Care Pastors have to fulfill their obligations in the care ministry. In the process I have repeatedly referred to Flocks (family groups) who receive the care but have not explained how they are assembled or how they are assigned to a Care Pastor. Of great importance is to note that Care Pastors do not have to find their own Flocks. The Care Leadership team, under the directive of the Care Director, make these allocations. When you complete the *CMNi* prescribed application form, you will have the opportunity to request up to three families of your own choosing. These will receive thoughtful consideration but are not guaranteed to be assigned to you. The final word rests with the leadership.

ASSIGNING FLOCKS TO CARE PASTORS

Care Pastors are not expected to solicit their own flocks. They are assigned to them. Assigning Flocks (family groups) to Care Pastors is an essential step in the process of implementing a care ministry network.

Never rush this critical function. Rather take your time and prayerfully select the people you think would relate best to the Care Pastor-couple you have in mind. It is always a good idea to run the final decisions by the Lead Pastor before any assignments are finalized — but allow the discretion to remain with theirs.

1. Start with geographic locations

It is best practice to initially assign Flocks to Care Pastors according to where they live. Suggestion: Divide your entire ministry-area into segments or areas according to the number of care pastors you have available. (E.g. if you have 25 Care Pastor-couples, divide your ministry area into twenty-five). Determine where your Care Pastors reside and place a pin (or use some software) where they live. Then assign those families who live closest to the Care Pastors as their Flock. This manner, however, is not a rule, but rather a safe starting point. Many times, relationships and interests dictate what's best, and should.

By segmenting your ministry-area into several areas, you will effectively be able to determine the number of families that live in such a given area This will help you determine how many families are left *uncared for* after the Flock assignments have been made. It will consequently also help you determine how many more Care Pastors still should be trained.

Most churches do not have enough care pastors initially. And that's okay. It is good practice to rather start small and expand, than begin too big and then have to scale down. The latter will create the impression that the ministry has failed.

2. Do not begin with the people on the periphery

When we initially introduced the care system, one church thought it to be a good way to draw people in from the periphery that were not closely knit into the church. They soon discovered that to be a huge mistake. The reason for this was that many of these marginal people did not regard the church as being their spiritual home and felt manipulated when they heard they were assigned to a Care Pastor. They, for the most part, responded very negatively when they were approached by someone they did not know and were offered a ministry they were quite frankly not interested in.

The truth was that many of those people were un-churched and had no interest of being involved in any form of ministry. Their names may have showed up after they attended a certain event, such as Baby Dedication, or an Easter or Christmas Production, or some other occasion, but never intended to become part of the church.

What was more startling to these people was the fact that, since they were not members of the congregation, had no idea what a Care Pastor was and why they would need them. They obviously had not heard the pastor cast the vision and neither had they learnt about the benefits of the care ministry.

Starting on the peripheral is the surest way of bringing mass discouragement to your Care Pastors and to all involved. It just will not work. After three short months, once excited Care Pastors, no longer were interested in the ministry. It took a whole lot of motivation for the momentum to kick back in for them.

My advice is, begin in Jerusalem — the household of faith - and then draw the circle further and further away. You will ultimately reach people out there, but the good thing is the church will then already have become very healthy and open to sincere friendships.

3. Family members

It is highly recommended that close family members not be assigned to a Care Pastor as flock members. This always turns out to become a challenge and takes away from the effectiveness of a church desiring to create a culture of care. If a Care Pastor, for instance, shows up at the bedside of his father (who is part of his flock) in hospital, he is not seen as a care pastor, but as his son — he was supposed to be there, it is family! It does not show that the pastor or church cares.

Now, reality beckons that when a church has been in existence for many years, people tend to inter-marry to the point where finally it appears the whole church is related. After I made the point of steering away from including family in a care pastor's flock at a training conference in a church, a lady raised her hand and said, "If that is how it's going to be, then we're in trouble. After all these years, we are all family!" The crowd roared with laughter at this reality. It was really funny!

If this should be the case in your church, it does not mean that this ministry cannot work, but it does mean that more discretion will have to be used. The church described above implemented the concept and it worked magnificently for them. As a matter of fact; it became a lifesaver to them. They assigned more-distant-family members to a Care Pastor as first choice and steered away from immediate, or very close family members. At the end of the day the pastor and leaders of a local congregation know their people and will know what works best.

4. Requests

As briefly mentioned before, Care Pastors will have an option to request up to three family units to be included in their Flock if they so desire. But do understand from the outset that all requests may not necessarily be honored but will be seriously considered — provided they are not personal family members.

A church in Florida chose to print the names and addresses of all the families in their database on index cards. They then "pinned" these to a large board in their fellowship hall on the night of the assignment. Care Pastors were then allowed to pick two families they knew from the board, and one family they did not know. They simply removed the selected cards from the board and wrote their own names on the reverse side and turned it in as directed. The Leadership Team then considered each of these requests and freely assigned two more family units from those cards that had remained on the board. This may be a viable option for you also. Just bear in mind that doing it this way could potentially mean that a selected family may live a distance from the Care Pastor and not in close proximity as when it is done geographically.

5. Making Changes

In most churches, we have found an initial, however minor, migration of families from one flock to another. We are comfortable with that process, if the same people don't keep on switching. Do not, however, *encourage* this to happen. Rather let things evolve by themselves.

Here is a point of caution: Once you have assigned people to a Care Pastor, and they are content, be very careful when you consider moving them to another flock afterward. The entire care concept is built on relationship and the more we can establish that principle, the better off we will be. In cases where families desire to change from one Care Pastor to another, it should be done in close cooperation with the Care Shepherd and Care Pastor.

It could be possible that the Leadership Team would want to balance the numbers of family groups per Care Pastor after they have made the initial allocations. Do not do this thoughtlessly. Once people have accepted their Care Pastor, they are usually not very eager to switch. Weigh the pros and the cons before making such changes.

6. Feeding the System

Although this is not the place to elaborate on it, we advise churches to have regular *membership conferences (classes)* where new members are allowed the opportunity to come into a covenant relationship with their church. New members commit to active participation while the church commits to nurturing and caring for them.[17]

During your new members conference (or however you may refer to it), you should clearly explain to the prospective church members that *pastoral care* in your congregation is provided through the *Care Ministry Network*. Explain to them that the Lead Pastor and other staff members will continue to provide *crisis care*, as they always have, but that ongoing congregational care is provided by qualified church members, called Care Pastors — *God's people taking care of one another.*

Apprise these new members that soon after they have been received into membership, each family will be assigned to an official Care Pastor. Describe briefly, yet clearly, how the care ministry functions and be sure to emphasize the reasons and benefits. Explain to them that it does not mean the Lead Pastor won't ever be involved with their lives, but it does mean that the pastor cares enough about each one of them, that he/she wants someone to be there for each member always.

---

17   Read more information concerning church membership in the *Care Revolution* in Chapter 9 on page 249.

Clarify that Care Pastors are not there to *replace* the pastor, but rather to *represent* the pastor. The *Care Ministry* is not meant to take away from, but rather to add on to accepted pastoral care.

It is essential that your care ministry culture is well described and clearly understood by new members before they agree to become part of the church. They should realize that the care concept is part of the congregation's DNA. It will avoid many questions later and make it much easier on the Care Pastors when they make the initial personal contact. When you clarify your method of congregational care to the new members, they readily accept the practice at the outset and therefore do not oppose the Care Pastors when they contact them (as is sometimes the case with established members).

After people have been accepted as members of the congregation, the Leadership Team assigns them to an appropriate Care Pastor-couple.

NETWORK GATHERINGS

To keep the Care Ministry relevant, fresh, and dynamic, it is necessary to have ongoing means of assembling your team. You will find that your *Care Ministry Network* will become more stable and effective when there is healthy interaction between the workers and leaders. It is for that reason that we have designed practical network gatherings which are essential for successful outcome.

You should be careful to never ever allow your Care Pastors/Shepherds to function in a vacuum, working on their own. It is the surest way of increasing attrition among them. When there is no meaningful interaction, they easily become prone to discouragement. It is when they hear of the victories, as well as even the struggles of their peers, that they get fresh wind in their sails. Let's face it; caring is easy, but it's not simple. When you work with real people you will always face challenges.

Our bulwark against discouragement and fatigue is by supporting one another through prayer and camaraderie. One of the many things I have learned from the African field is that the solitary deer becomes the easiest prey to a hungry lion. But when they stay in the group, they are protected by each other. In our times together, as we enjoy fellowship, we receive new strength and nerve to continue in this important task. New information and helpful tools give us newfound energy and motivates us to continue with new vigor. There is wisdom in the counsel of many. The manner of these gatherings is fundamentally a discipleship process for the entire care ministry workforce.

Taking the Lead

These network gatherings fall under the leadership of the Director and the Leadership Team. Although the Lead Pastor is not expected to be there, it is a good idea if he/she would show up from time to time, even if it were only a short greeting or word of encouragement.

Besides the training conference and personal meetings between Care Shepherds and Care Pastors, it is essential that all involved in the Care Ministry attend the prescribed gatherings for harmony, synchronization, fellowship, and ongoing training.

1. Monthly Fellowship

The purpose of the monthly fellowship is to stay in touch with each other and to maintain progress within the network among the care shepherds and care pastors. The more cohesive your workers are, the more effective the ministry will function. Although everyone may not be able to attend every monthly meeting, it should however, never be presented as being optional.

The Monthly Fellowship does not have to be lengthy and can sometimes be conducted around any other regularly scheduled church meeting: before the mid-week service, or after Sunday am service, or whatever works best. This meeting should normally not take more than about a half-hour to one hour, so be very prudent and well organized. Knowing the heart and reading the pulse of where the ministry is and what is transpiring, the director and leaders should determine what to emphasize during each of these monthly meetings.

Sometimes informative, short instruction should be included; at another, strong encouragement and motivation should be the order of the meeting. At other times, joyous feedback and positive reports should hold the floor. Be flexible and remain innovative, and make sure you don't fall into a rut and make these gathering monotonous. Never let your teams feel they are wasting their time or get the impression that this meeting is trivial or of little significance.

The Monthly Fellowship is the place and time for the leaders to inform Care Shepherds/Pastors of what is happening in the church-at-large and to share some of the exciting things to come (special function, pastor's sermon series, and more). This shared information should contain general events of the church and not be restricted to only care ministry events. Offering these details provides Care Pastors with the particulars they will need to share with their flocks during their monthly phone contacts.

At times when calendars and seasons are packed, and physical meetings cannot readily take place, the Leadership Team must ensure that pertinent information is at least sent through emails or other electronic communications to those who could not attend. Some churches follow through by utilizing the most attractive full color newsletters for this purpose.

ADDED ADVANTAGE: A further great benefit of having an established network such as the Care Ministry Network is that information can be shared in a personal way with everyone in the congregation in a short span of time — from the leaders all the way down to each member. In times of emergencies (when powerlines can be down), weather alerts, event cancellations, catastrophes, and more, word can be released from the leadership, and through the levels of leadership, can reach people wherever they may find themselves. All it takes is for everyone involved to just call those whom they are responsible for. Each one just makes a few calls and within a short span of time information can be shared with the entire congregation.

2. Quarterly Summit

Continuing education is imperative to the ongoing success of the Care Ministry and the *Quarterly Summit* is the event that is utilized for this purpose. Training and development should be at the heart of this summit. Things change so rapidly that we should stay on top of it always. The subject of *caring* is also so wide that we can never exhaust all the information. The more we know, the better equipped we will be to do our work effectively. The *Quarterly Summit* is best presented in seminar format. Food, although not required, is always an important catalyst.

This meeting should preferably be conducted on a Saturday morning when it can be presented in a more relaxed, and not rushed, atmosphere. Bearing in mind that this gathering only takes place four times a year, ample time should be allotted. Three hours seems to be the average time churches are devoting to this event. During this *Quarterly Summit*, all Care Shepherds/Pastors and their assistants should come together to receive further instruction and be refreshed for the next few months ahead.

Although times of fellowship should be included, *teaching* must be at the core of this gathering and should be the focus. Prepare notes and outlines for all present and make it a beneficial time of learning. Any course correction should be done during these meetings. By this time, I'm sure that all involved will understand why we said at the outset that Care Pastors should preferably limit their involvement in other ministries. Providing meaningful care is time consuming, especially if we desire to remain on the cutting edge.

The actual teaching done during the *Quarterly Summit* can be done by the Lead Pastor, a Staff member, the Care Director, members of the Leadership Team, or even a guest speaker. Make sure all Care Shepherds/Pastors have a sturdy three-ring binder to retain all their notes. This adds value to the gatherings and gives importance to the note-outlines given, but even more so, becomes a valuable and organized ready-reference tool for the future. Should you require content to include in your training, contact CMNi Central. You may also utilize one of their consultants, should you so desire.

It is always a good idea to do something special for the workers at these meetings. Sometimes an appropriate book or devotional may be a good idea. Be innovative in making your event meaningful and be sure to serve refreshments also. If you are going to extend your meeting close to or over the lunch hour, be sure to provide a light lunch. Care Shepherds and Care Pastors are worth the effort and the expense.

3. Annual Celebration

This meeting should be at the end of your ministry year — one year after you have launched the ministry. Avoid having it at the end of the calendar year since there are already so many other functions taking place at Christmas time. An evening over a weekend seems most appropriate for this occasion.

The *Annual Celebration* should always be a time of celebrating the good things the Lord has done, as well as the exciting things that have happened through the care network over the past twelve months. Let it be a time of rejoicing and thanksgiving.

This is the proper time to celebrate the Care Shepherds/Pastors and their assistants. Show gratitude to them for their ministry, love, devotion, and sacrifice. Give them feedback reports of the work they had done and state clearly the positive results of their ministry to the congregation. It is also a great idea to solicit some church members to come in and testify of the great work their care pastors had done.

Fun, fellowship and celebration should be at the order of the day. This is normally not a time for instruction or education. *Throw a party* instead! Invite the Lead Pastor and all other pastors and ministry leaders to the occasion. Include all elements — food, cakes, pies, beverages, desserts, etc.! Make it a joy-filled gathering, although not frivolous or silly.

This is also a suitable time to bid farewell to those who will not be continuing in the ministry and welcoming potential care pastors who have been approved to serve in this capacity in the future.

The creativity of this event is left to the imagination and innovation of the Director and Leadership Team. Make it huge; make your pastor proud, and let God be glorified!

Protocols

Our premise of creating a care ministry network is to relieve the pastor of routine congregational care and instead allow members to care for one another. With that in mind we do not want to over-burden the pastor with additional training responsibilities either. It is therefore the responsibility of the Care Director and Leadership Team to organize and structure these network gatherings. Many times, leaders ask who should be teaching these meetings and who should select potential care pastors. Our response to that is basically the following:

1. There are of course no set rules. Each church decides its own practices - and church-size seems to be the determining factor.
2. In smaller churches the pastor seems to stay much more connected to the Care Ministry than would be the case for larger churches. What we do however state emphatically, in all cases, is that the pastor should never let go of the ministry in its entirety. The level of the pastor's involvement remains his/her own prerogative but if the pastor totally relinquishes the ministry, it will eventually wane and most likely vanish. The Care Director is the extension of the pastor, not the replacement.
3. Since "caring" touches the nerve of pastoring, it speaks for itself that the pastor should be kept in the loop when selecting potential care pastors. The Care Director should be involved in recommending new leaders, but the pastor should have input in the final selection. The same applies to assigning families to care pastors. (As a helpful suggestion people should best not know they are being considered as prospective new care leaders during the selection process, so they will not feel slighted when not invited).
4. Regarding the ongoing training of Care Shepherds and Care Pastors, the Care Director can do the actual

training, or utilize other people, as mentioned before. Some churches have Care Directors that can teach, others don't. Should the pastor desire to be involved in training, it should remain his/her choice. I personally think the latter is great, especially at times during the Quarterly Summits. Include the Care Director but not necessarily exclusively. Let giftedness be the determining factor. I find that most pastors stay involved with at least some form of training - this connection breeds content.

THE COMMISSIONING SERVICE

You may have read or heard somewhere that we refer to the act of *commissioning* and may have wondered what it meant. Well, here is what it's all about.

After Care Pastors have completed the training conference and have passed through the qualifying process, they should be officially introduced and appointed to their ministry role. The ideal, and most effective way of fulfilling this act of commissioning is by doing so in the presence of the entire congregation.

The Commissioning of Care Pastors should not be regarded as being superfluous or even optional. This service is the only way whereby your Care Pastors are publicly recognized and openly authorized to function in their roles which is actually vital. If done correctly, it could become a highlight in the life of your church. I like what one church did. They gave each of their Care Pastors a white towel as part of the commissioning to indicate that this ministry is not about a title, but rather about a towel - a clear symbol of servitude.

Make the service a consecrated moment of dedication as you acknowledge and dedicate the Care Pastors as able ministers within the Body. It is this public assignment and act of entrustment that gives them the official authority to function within the congregation. Simultaneously, it becomes a perfect moment for the members to accept them as such. This ceremony is to the Care Pastors, what credentialing is to the clergy. It gives them the right to serve in their capacity as servant-leaders. Avoiding this formality will make it increasingly more difficult for your Care Pastors to function effectively in their respective roles.

NOTE: As part of the service, it will be appropriate to apprise the congregation of the equipping and training process these candidates underwent to earn their qualifications. Clarify that these individuals are responding to a call of God and have chosen to be equipped for the work of the ministry within the boundaries of the local church. They are willing to set themselves apart to care for the wellbeing of their fellow congregants.

The Lead Pastor and other Elders should *commission* the Care Pastors — preferably during a Sunday morning service for the greatest impact. Each Care Pastor should be anointed with oil, hands lain on them and through this act, be authorized publicly to serve in their role as a Care Pastor.

Some churches have designed their *Commissioning Service* to be something like a graduation ceremony, complete with caps and gowns. Now you don't have to do any of these things, but you do need to put every effort forward to conduct a commissioning ceremony and making it special. The attention you give to this event also emphasizes to the congregation the value you as pastor place on the Care Ministry and underscores its value. This is simply a moment not to miss.

Through conducting a *Commissioning Service,* you most likely may also be releasing motivation for potential care pastors to enlist. "If old Joe and Suzie can do this, I know we can do it too!" may very well be the common thread of people's thinking.

Acknowledge those
who work hard among you,
who care for you in the Lord.

CERTIFICATES AND NAMETAGS

Certificates
Commissioned Care Pastors should each receive an official *Certificate of Completion* with their personal names inscribed on it. You will be absolutely amazed to see the response of people when they receive these certificates. It's not only about a piece of paper, it's rather an act of publicly legitimizing and recognizing the individual.

Nametags
Each one should also receive a professional looking *nametag* (badge) that identifies him or her as a *Care Pastor*, along with his or her own name engraved on the badge as well. These are to be worn at **every** church and ministry occasion. Do make sure these nametags are not cheap or tacky looking. We used pin-attached brass "badges" with the names engraved on it of each Care Pastor at our church. Make the nametags look professional.

10

ACTING PROFESSIONALLY

It is not required of members to have formal education or professional qualifications as a prerequisite to function as Care Pastors. People's giftedness and credentials come from the Holy Spirit and their authority from the local church leadership. They should, however, be equipped, developed, and trained before they can function alongside their pastor to provide quality congregational care.

Although Care Pastors are not professionals, they perform a ministry that requires *professionalism*. We need to, however, distinguish between *being* professional and being *a* professional. There is a difference. "Being professional" means performing a task with excellence in an exceptional way. Care Pastors should always view their ministry as *being* professional rather than being *a* professional, which they are not.

Our goal for the Care Ministry is: Doing all things with excellence and doing it all to God's Glory!

When we consider the aspect of professionalism in ministry, the first thing that comes to mind is the matter of integrity. This defines who we are. To possess integrity is to be incapable of compromising that which we believe to be true. A person of integrity adheres to moral and ethical principles even when their actions cannot be seen by others. Integrity means we remain consistent, loyal, and trustworthy under all circumstances and that we will never surrender our principles whatever the cost. A person simply cannot minister effectively as a Care Pastor if there is a lack of veracity.

Being precedes *doing*. *Who you are* as a Care Pastor is more important than *what you do* in ministry. Being effective in caring for others becomes effortless when it flows from who you truly are on the inside. As a Care Pastor you must *be* a person of proven character before you can *do* the ministry of caring. When we spend more time in positively developing our ethics and attitudes, we will become much more effective in developing reliable relationships.

Professional Functions

Since the idea of church members functioning as Care Pastors is fairly new, many may not know exactly what to do, what to avoid, what is expected, and what to accept as normal. In this chapter we are giving more direction to the functioning role of a Care Pastor when expected to act professionally.

The following quotes may prove very helpful for members-in-training to know how to conduct themselves in their ministry-role. Although these are not necessarily verbatim, I have taken most phrases from Mel Steinbron's book, "Can the Pastor do it Alone?"[18]

---

18   Melvin J. Steinbron, *Can the Pastor do it Alone.* Wipf and Stock, Eugene, OR, 2004. P95.

1. **Be yourself.** Do not try to be like someone else, especially your pastor or one of the staff persons. It will make you feel insecure and people will notice. Minister in your own style, using your own words, and your own expressions.
2. **Be human.** Being a Care Pastor does not mean you have to now act overly spiritual. Genuinely care for people without squelching your spontaneous self.
3. **Stay focused.** Most conversations start with small talk but stay focused on your purpose for being with the person(s) you're meeting with and get down to business. Deal with the crisis; give encouragement; ask the questions that will bring problems and joys to the surface; show your faith and your life; make time to pray.
4. **Know what you are doing.** Although you have been trained, you will not become a perfect Care Pastor, but you can love, and you can use the skills you have acquired thus far. When talking with people, don't be intimidated because you may think they have some qualifications you don't. Realize that you have been trained in ways *they* have not. So, go ahead and put into practice what you have learned.
5. **Use your proper authority.** Do not disavow the authority given you by the Lord and your church to pastor on their behalf. Your demeanor should build people's confidence in you. You represent Christ and your pastor, and you are called to function in your role.

6. **Be dependable.** You need to follow through on what you say you are going to do. When you cannot follow through on an appointment, call the people to tell them why you cannot be there or why you will be late.
7. **Be available in case of emergency.** Your dedication to your people will require that you make yourself available to them. Be willing to be on call at all hours, just like a physician. Sometimes it is just your presence that is needed. Being available means your people know how to reach you.
8. **Be assertive.** You are available, but you are not a servant in the sense of responding to every beck and call. If you think you are being manipulated, deal with it by being able to say no and yes appropriately. Never be forced into performing what you have not been assigned to do.
9. **Know your limitations.** No one has all the answers. When necessary, refer your people to those who have professional qualifications or who you believe are more competent than you for that particular problem. You are equipped to provide congregational care, not crisis care. E.g. if you are asked if a family should turn off the life-support of a loved one at a hospital, refer the matter to your Care Shepherd or your pastor. It now falls into the category of crisis care.
10. **Be forgiving of yourself.** You will make mistakes and feely badly about them. You cannot expect to be perfect. Evaluate the causes for the mistakes, learn from them to avoid similar mistakes in the future and then

forgive yourself. "To err is human, to forgive is divine" applies to forgiving yourself as well as others.

A Matter of Counseling

The Care Ministry Network does not cover the aspect of counseling and therefore undeniably stresses that Care Pastors should not seek to provide counseling of any kind. It is simply not your role and neither have you been trained for it. You should be very careful to never refer to yourself as a counselor and likewise never attempt to perform such acts. You are free to share Biblical principles and provide spiritual direction to people who need help.

During your times of ministry, people will present problems and challenges to you, asking your advice, or solicit your opinion. It's okay to hear them out, but then offer your support in prayer, both in the moment as well as futuristic, instead of attempting to help solve their problem. Depending on the severity of the situation, you should refer the matter to your upline to gain direction. Follow up later with the individual (or family) to assure the matter has been resolved.

There are way too many pitfalls in the matter of counseling for us to attempt solving complicated issues. Remember, you are called to pastoral care not professional counseling.

Confidentiality

After having dealt with the subject of counseling it seems appropriate for me to also address the subject of confidentiality. It is an integral part of a Care Pastor's responsibility and becomes one of the essential foundation pieces of a healthy relationship.

Summary: Confidentiality is the obligation not to disclose willingly any information obtained in confidence. Someone once said that even a fish wouldn't get caught if it kept its mouth shut! Confidentiality is a gift to be shared in the privacy of prayer.

It is only when a person has confidence in you as a Care Pastor that he or she will find freedom to express personal thoughts and feelings with you. Confidentiality builds trust, honest communication, and openness. When your people view you as a person in whom they can confide, they will make you the custodian of their inner most feelings. They are extending a special gift of trust to you. Whatever you do, never break that confidentiality. Never betray their trust. You will never have a second chance to regain it.

As relationships with your people grow and develop, you are going to find that they may share with you some serious private things concerning their personal lives and circumstances. At those moments, be a good listener, but then determine to guard their privacy with your life. Confidentiality is a serious matter which is built over time and is earned, never deserved. Don't take it lightly and never ever squander this treasure.

"The glory of friendship is not the outstretched hand, not the kindly smile, nor the joy of companionship; it is the spiritual inspiration that comes to one when you discover that someone else believes in you and is willing to trust you with a friendship."

– *Ralph Waldo Emerson.*

Confidentiality in a Pastoral Relationship

As could be understood, there are different levels of confidentiality. Although both should be respected, there's a difference between things that could be regarded as public knowledge and those that are deemed private knowledge. *Public knowledge* includes those matters which are known by other people or could be made known without breaching any privacy. *Private knowledge*, on the other hand, refers to information that is not generally known by others or at least should not be made known.

When there is doubt, the best part of wisdom is to check with the individual and get permission before information is shared. Rather err on the side of being overly cautious than being overly talkative. The golden rule in a pastoral relationship is: Whether public or private, do not become the newscaster. Wisdom may say, "Leave it alone, and just pray!"

Thoughtfulness: Because of the ministry role you are functioning in, some people may approach you and ask you to share information of someone in your ministry-group. They may even do so under the guise that they want to know "how to best pray for them." Do not be tempted to breach your people's confidence. If someone has a burden for one of your families, encourage them to pray for them by name in fervent prayer. God knows the need.

One Final Point: In some very rare cases you may run across certain forms of abuse as you work with people. Although we will not deal with this matter in-depth, we need to draw your attention to the fact that there is no confidentiality when abuse or neglect, as defined by state law, occurs with children or the elderly. Failure to report these cases to the proper authorities may result in criminal and/or civil liability.

Brad Hambrick, the pastor of counseling at the Summit Church in North Carolina, defines abuse as follows:

- Inflicting or allowing non-accidental, serious physical injury

- Creating or allowing a substantial risk of non-accidental, serious physical injury
- Using or allowing cruel or grossly inappropriate procedures or devices to modify behavior
- Committing, permitting, or encouraging the rape of the child or other sexual crimes
- Creating or allowing serious emotional damage to the child
- Encouraging, directing, or approving delinquent acts involving moral turpitude committed by the child

Pastors are also expected to report neglect based on these criteria:
- Does not receive proper care, supervision, or discipline
- Abandonment
- Not provided necessary medical care
- Lives in an environment injurious to the child's welfare
- Has been placed for care or adoption in violation of the law

Hambrick warns that many may fail in their reporting responsibilities because they're unsure if abuse truly occurred. But he points out that a "reasonable suspicion" is all that the law requires, and the authorities don't expect pastors or others to be investigators. They have trained social workers to vet the charges. When abuse is against an adult, the abuse victim is granted the choice of pressing charges or not.[19]

---

19 http//: links churchleaders.com - January 25, 2019. Here's What You Need to Know About Reporting Abuse.

The Art of Listening

During your ministry as a Care Pastor you will find *listening* to be one of the most important demands for being effective. The truth, however, is that listening is more difficult than most people realize. We have often heard it said: "there's a huge difference between hearing and listening." James 1:9 says, "Understand this, my dear brothers and sisters: You must all be quick to listen, slow to speak . . ."

> *A wise old owl lived in an oak,*
> *The more he saw the less he spoke*
> *The less he spoke the more he heard.*
> *Why can't we all be like that wise old bird?*
> — *Author unknown*

All of us have spent years to learn how to read, write, and count, but for the most part have never really learnt how to *listen*. It will do all of us good to learn how to listen more and speak less. The fact that God gave us two ears and one mouth should tell us something. When we listen to people, it clearly shows that we honor them and value what they have to say.

What is important in the art of listening is to develop the discipline of listening instead of preparing to answer. "Most people do not listen with the intent to understand; they listen with the intent to reply"- Stephen R. Covey. It is for that reason that so many misunderstandings occur when we are trying to communicate — even in marriage relationships.

Once you have mastered the skill of being a good listener you will quickly also learn to appreciate that there are great rewards and valuable paybacks to be gained from your efforts. We can listen to

500 or 600 words per minute but can only speak about 150 words per minute. That means we have ample time to think while we are listening.

Some Principles of Good Listening

1. **Pay Attention.** You will never be able to listen if your mind is wandering. In fact, if you are not paying attention, you are not listening. At an unexpected moment the speaker may ask for a response and if you do not act appropriately the communication is over. He or she will know you are not listening. Don't miss valuable information by letting your mind wander.
2. **Look the Person in the Eyes.** Never create the habit of looking over their shoulder. It creates the impression that you are seeking someone more important to talk to and that you don't really care about them or what they have to say. It can sometimes be hard to unlearn this behavior.
3. **Make Sure You Can Hear the Person.** If you cannot hear what is being said, listening becomes impossible. If the environment is not conducive to hearing, move location if possible, but make every effort to be able to clearly hear the conversation.
4. **Ask Questions.** Do not interrupt the person, but at appropriate moments, ask sensible questions. In this way the speaker will know you are paying attention and listening. Asking good questions is the key to effective communication. Show your genuine concern.
5. **Participate.** This is best done by nodding your head while the other person is speaking, smiling, or even

sometimes by expressing your understanding with a slight frown of the brow. Being a good listener does not mean you turn into a statue or something. Feel free to say things like, "Uh-huh" "Yes" "Sure" "Okay". Show interest in what they are saying. And, of course, never glance at your watch during the conversation.

6. **Listen for What is Not Being Said.** Sometimes these are more important than what IS being said. Listen for those things that are being repeated during the conversation — that may be the essence of the discussion. Watch body language (crossed arms, frowns, etc.)

7. **Repeat the Words Being Used.** Using the words and phrases of the speaker illustrates your careful attention to detail and honors their forms and means of expression.

Communication

Our ministry concept is built on the premise of developing healthy relationships; the principle key for accomplishing this is through meaningful communication.

Listening is the first step in effective communication, but good communication requires more than basic listening — it requires a response before it can be evaluated. There is a definite cycle that needs to be completed before communication can be accepted as having been effective:

1. Sender. There first has to be a sender — someone that speaks, writes, or even signals.
2. Recipient. Someone must receive the message.

3. Channel. The message can be transmitted in written form, verbally, or non-verbally such as hand signals, facial expressions, body language, etc.
4. Message. Of course, there has to be a message that is sent.
5. Understanding. The message has to be understood by the receiver.
6. Response. Communication is never complete until there is some form of response (feedback) from the recipient back to the sender.

People remember:
- 10% of what they read
- 20% of what they hear
- 30% of what they see
- 40% of what they hear and see.

I know that you believe you understand what you think I said, but I'm not sure you realize that what you heard is not what I meant (Robert McCloskey).

Effective Communication
- Don't try to tell your own "bigger than life" story.
- Don't let your talking overtake your listening.
- Don't always exude the negative.
- Don't let your mouth overrule your mind. Think before you speak.
- Don't ignore personal hygiene.

Developing Your Spiritual Health

There can hardly be any better way to develop your character and your integrity, than to develop your spirit being. As a Care Pastor it will serve you well to spend time in cultivating meaningful spiritual dynamics in your life. The more time you spend with God, the easier it will be to reach out to people. Accept at the outset that developing spiritual health is never a completed task; for the Care Pastor the school is never out. It will require of you to spend private time with God, not only to be able to minister, but rather to personally grow into spiritual maturity.

There are primarily two ways to develop your spiritual health:
1. Spending Time with God.
2. Developing a Relationship with the Holy Spirit.

1. Spending Time with God

Time spent with God is the single most important discipline in the life of an effective Care Pastor. The more time we spend with Him, the more we will become like Him. It is like in marriage — the longer a couple is married, the more they begin to act like each other — they even begin to think like each other. It's the relationship that creates the image.

If you want to be a servant, you must know your Master. We need to linger a little longer in the presence of God, so His nature can be imparted into us and we are able to hear His voice.

1.1 Reading His Word

It will be of little value if we spend all our time serving others and neglect our personal time of reading the Word for our own benefit and spiritual enrichment. Take time to deposit as much as possible of the Word into your spirit so you may have enough invested when the time comes to withdraw.

The central purpose of reading or studying the Bible is neither to achieve doctrinal purity nor to amass information, but to effect "inner transformation".
— Richard Foster

Five ways of benefitting from the Word:
1. Hear the Word
2. Read the Word
3. Study the Word
4. Memorize the Word
5. Meditate on the Word

A Care Pastor who desires to truly reflect the image of God in his or her pastoral work will always refer to the Bible as their reference for both, truth and instruction. Allow the Word of God to remain your firm foundation. Everything you do must be a reflection of what the Bible says. When you digest the Word according to the five above disciplines, you will acquire a wealth of wisdom and have ample resources to share with your family groups.

1.2 Prayer

Spending time with God certainly includes taking time to pray. This should be a high priority on the list of any person who desires to be involved in ministry. While it is a requirement for Care Pastors to pray regularly for their people, they should not only be praying for others, but also utilize the time to worship God in spirit and in truth for their own personal growth. Prayer is communicating with God. Learn how to simply speak to God as you would to a close friend. Time given in prayer is never wasted. Develop a rhythm for your prayer life, because it is the heartbeat of your spiritual life.

Prayer changes the pray-er!

Some Helpful Thoughts on Prayer

When you pray:
- Pray with fervency (James 5:16).
- Pray with persistence (Luke 18:1-7).
- Pray over personal needs.
- Pray for pastoral relationships.
- Pray for personal and family relationships
- Pray for your leaders.

Dr. Jerry Kirk said, *"When I am not praying as I should, I am not pastoring as I should."*

This may be a good place to underscore to Care Pastors, and all others involved in this ministry, that you have been called forth as a minister within your local congregation to serve in a very responsible position. Never assume that your engagements with your people are simply mechanical actions. You have been entrusted with a special gift — God's Family. For that reason, and many others, you should be prepared spiritually to serve with an attitude of surrender and gratitude.

"As for me, I will call upon God, And the LORD shall save me. Evening and morning and at noon I will pray, and cry aloud, And He shall hear my voice." Psalm 55:16-17. (NKJV)

2. Developing a Relationship with the Holy Spirit

When it comes to congregational care, the leadership of the Holy Spirit is crucial. Both the human and divine participate in caring for the saints. As a Care Pastor, you fill the role of the human. The Holy Spirit is the divine. It is the Holy Spirit who gives us the power to do ministry (Acts 1:8). It is futile to think we can do any kind of work in the Kingdom of God without the power of the Holy Spirit.

The Bible says in John 14:16,17 that He is *with* and *in* the believer. Ephesians 5:18 instructs us to *"Be filled with the Spirit."* This statement Paul made was written in the continuing tense and should read, "Be ye, **being** filled with the Spirit," which in a simple sense means, "continue to be filled with the Spirit" or "be constantly filled with the Spirit." The reason for this is so that we can be ready to function in our ministry role at all times. These directives are not meant to highlight some denominational position but actually speak to every follower of Christ, regardless of doctrinal persuasion.

Before Jesus ascended into heaven, He gave the disciples well-defined instruction of the work and necessity of the Holy Spirit in the life of every believer. He stated very clearly the work the Spirit will do in our lives. (Read John chapters 14 through 16).

The Work of The Holy Spirit

The Holy Spirit gives us:
1. Power to do ministry

2. Gifts for pastoring
3. Discernment for effectiveness
4. Revelation to understand
5. Wisdom to know what to do, and
6. Guidance how to pray.
   - Luke tells us that the Holy Spirit gives us God's power to minister and witness. (Luke 24:48,49; Acts 1:8).
   - Paul, in writing about the Holy Spirit, says He both brings us into the family of God and enables inner growth at the same time. (Romans 8:9-11; 1Corinthians 12:4-11).
   - The Care Ministry Network provides the structure to utilize people's gifts they have received from the Holy Spirit. It is one of the forms that Christ uses to make His Spirit working and available and present with people.

Stir up the Gift of God

It is vitally important to develop (stir up) the Spiritual Gifts we have received from God. If we neglect to do so they become dormant and our ministries become ineffective. Paul admonishes his spiritual son, Timothy, "Therefore I remind you to stir up the gift of God which is in you . . ." (2 Timothy 1:6). We maximize our gifts when we are equipped and implement them within the body of Christ.

A Care Pastor should be very sensitive to the leadership of the Holy Spirit when ministering to people in personal contact, phone calls, home appointments, hospital visits, and more. Allow the Holy Spirit to give you wisdom and discernment as you continually pray for your flock. Listen to His feintest whisper because His revelation is more valuable than most other helps you can ever find.

The Holy Spirit will not only give you revelation, but also the necessary boldness, courage, and strength to function effectively in your calling. Remember: He is the One who is in you and walks besides you. He is the *Paraclete,* the *Comforter.*

Always check on the depth of your fullness of the Holy Spirit and be sure to be constantly filled. Allow Him to lead you in every step of your life. If you try to run on empty, *burnout* will be a definite result! You will suffer, your flock members will suffer, and so will the body of Christ. Attempting to provide ministry in your own ability will most always result in you quitting the ministry. A Care Pastor, filled with the power and love of Jesus Christ, will always be capable of ministering to a hurting member in his or her flock.

"Without God we cannot;
without us He will not!"
— *Augustine*

11

KEEPING THE VISION ALIVE

One of the most important, and sometimes challenging aspects of the care ministry, is to keep the vision alive before the congregation. The danger is that the care ministry could potentially blend so much into the daily operations of the congregation that it could gradually become another program. That should never be allowed to happen. Providing effective care to members at all times should remain a priority to pastors, leaders, and church members alike. The vision must be kept alive. Once a pastor has motivated the congregation to commit to the culture of care, their responsibility as leaders will be to maintain integrity by not allowing the ministry to wane. Should the vision ever diminish it will cause a vacuum that cannot be easily filled in any other way.

Suggested Ways of Keeping the Vision Alive
1. **Publications.** Continually publish the care ministry events in all the church's marketing media — newsletters, bulletins, websites, and everywhere else.

2. **Video Clips.** Produce short video clips (simply using an iPhone and computer) from members, Care Pastors, etc., and add it to some Sunday announcements. It adds much more to the effectiveness of promotions. (Do not show every Sunday. It gets boring. But do keep them coming).
3. **Care Ministry Newsletter.** Create a monthly newsletter aimed at all those involved in the care ministry. Keep them updated on all relevant matters in the congregation as well as exciting things happening in the care ministry. Use this to also mention the celebrations of the Care Shepherds/Pastors — birthdays, anniversaries, graduation, etc. It also serves as a good platform to remind them of upcoming care ministry events.
4. **Personal Testimonies.** Selectively have people share publicly what they have encountered through the care ministry. There's nothing more powerful than hearing first-hand accounts of people's experiences of what the care ministry means to them. When you allow your congregation to hear the blessing others have received, the reality of the ministry will confidently hit home.
5. **During Messages.** Discreetly mention from time to time, some of the blessings of the care ministry during your Sunday messages to the congregation. It will validate what the care ministers are accomplishing.
6. **Banners.** Display professionally designed, colorful banners and posters around the church building, promoting the *Care Ministry Network*. Do so especially

during the launch of the ministry and the recruiting of people to attend the training conference. Repeat this again when you plan another training event and thus want more people to become involved.

7. **Badges.** Do not underestimate the value of Care Shepherds/Pastors, wearing their lapels pins (or badges) during all church events — not only Sundays. They become like walking "billboards".

8. **Marketing Concepts.** It's a very good idea to have tee-shirts and golf shirts made available to those involved in your care ministry. Wearing them at church events keeps the ministry before the people. They too become like walking "billboards". People are often curious and want to know more about the tops the care pastors wear. It creates a great opportunity to talk about the purpose of the Care Ministry Network. Some ministries have also provided coffee mugs with the care ministry logo on it to be used in their church's coffee shop.

Final Word

In this book I have attempted to provide in detail the relevant steps for preparing the members and launching your church for an effective *Care Ministry Network*. When reading through the entire book, it appears the implementation of this ministry could be overwhelming and very cumbersome. To that I will agree if you just read all the information as you would a novel.

That is, however, not the case when you begin to roll out the concept one step at a time.

The purpose of this publication should not be viewed as the principles, philosophies, and theology of the *Care Ministry Network*.

Those things are covered in my book, *The Care Revolution,* which I highly suggest you read, if you have not yet done so. That book will give you much more insight into the background and Biblical foundation of the necessity of engaging a care ministry in your congregation.

The *Handbook* was prepared as a resource to help pastors and churches to easily be able to implement the care ministry. My intent is for you to realize that you don't have to wonder how to get the job done, but instead realize that all the work has been done for you already. Just follow the steps meticulously. It is for that reason that I described every step with much detail, probably at times more than should be necessary.

In addition to the step-by-step instructions, I have also provided all the relevant tools a church may need in terms of supplemental material such as sermon outlines, sample letters, job descriptions, certificates, and so much more. All these have been professionally designed and are yours simply for downloading and utilizing. You have the right to edit them the way you want.

The *Handbook* is also meant to become a ready reference tool for ongoing development and constant reference — especially when questions arise. This is especially helpful after the training conference when everyone discovers their own uncertainties and would want to know what to do or how to handle a specific situation. That of necessity would mean that all involved should have their own copy of the *Handbook.*

In the past, we provided training to local churches only by means of conferences personally presented by one of our team members, which is still available. (Contact us for more information). Doing it that way, most of the answers were potentially provided by a consultant and subsequently filled the vacuum. The *Handbook* intends to be the practical and ongoing *alternative* for these live events, although we still recommend utilizing the service of one of our consultants for the first training conference. The *Handbook* should still be used, even if you do engage our team for equipping purposes.

CLOSING THOUGHTS

The Care Revolution Process

The Care Revolution is an all-encompassing process of development which helps pastors and churches establish a workable care ministry system in their churches. Since the traditional way of providing pastoral care no longer works, it has become necessary to implement the Biblical pattern of empowering church members to partner with their pastors to provide ongoing care to one another. "That the members should have the same care for one another." 1 Corinthians 12:25

The Care Revolution has three stages of development:
1. The *Care Revolution* textbook
2. *The Care Revolution Handbooks*
3. The *Care Revolution* training guides

THE CARE REVOLUTION TEXTBOOK

The *Care Revolution* textbook is a 379-page book which describes the principles, philosophy, and theology of a practical care system. It deals extensively with the need of such a system and fully describes how the problem arose, the origin of the Great Commitment as the solution, the Biblical undergirding of congregational care, the behavior of humankind in a modern era, the crisis we face in pastoral care, the role of Lead Pastors, discovering, developing, and deploying of Spiritual Gifts, and so much more.

THE CARE MINISTRY HANDBOOK

*Care Ministry Handbook*s are written to help pastors, leaders, and church members to easily launch and maintain an effective Care Ministry Network in the local church. Pastors are not left to struggle on their own trying to decipher the best ways of implementation. All the work has already been done. It describes the levels of leadership, how to develop a functionable system of care, the easy-to-follow contact system, and fully describes step-by-step, the easy to understand phases of unfolding the care ministry. The *Handbook for Pastors and Leaders* includes a practical Addendum section that provides numerous tools for churches to utilize in their application. It provides the launching steps, job descriptions of each level, sermon outlines, model letters, and many more helpful and relevant material.

THE TRAINING GUIDES

Taken out of the above-mentioned publications, the Training Guides have been designed as helpful tools to train and equip church members during the *Care Pastors Training Conference*. Throughout these guides, references are made back to the *Care Revolution Textbook* (C.R.) and the *Handbook* (H.B.) for clear understanding of the concept. These guides are required for the training and preparation of potential Care Pastors and come prepared as (1) A Facilitator's Guide, and (2) As a Participant's Guide. Equipping church members without these guides come close to being impossible. Not only are these guides most helpful for equipping Care Pastors but also becomes their ongoing, personal reference manual as they develop their own ministry.

ON OUR WEBSITE YOU CAN:

1. Order the *Care Revolution textbook*
2. Order further copies of the *Care Revolution Handbooks.*
3. Order the *Care Pastors Training Guides,* which include the *Facilitator's Guide* and the *Participant's Guide.*
4. Download the Addendum Material Package found in the *Handbook for Pastors and Leaders:*
   4.1. Appendix A – The Sermon Outlines
   4.2. Appendix B – Prepatory Material
   4.3. Appendix C – The Launch
   4.4. Appendix D – The Commissioning Service
   4.5. Appendix E – The Job Descriptions of each level
   4.6. Appendix F – Sample Letters
   4.7. Appendix G – The Application Form for care Pastors
   4.8. Appendix H – The Official Certificate
   4.9. Appendix J – The Promotional Pamphlet.

Each of the abovementioned four categories can be ordered separately. There is a nominal fee for the download material.

OUR WEBSITE: www.cmni.org

www.ingramcontent.com/pod-product-compliance
Lightning Source LLC
Chambersburg PA
CBHW030326100526
44592CB00010B/583